LIBERTY ON LIFE SUPPORT

Essays on American Exceptionalism,
Immigration, Education, and the Economy

DR. ILEANA JOHNSON PAUGH

DEDICATION

I dedicate this book to my patient husband David, whose love and technology guidance are priceless. He is and will always be my research and writing enabler.

I will be remiss in not mentioning my beautiful Snowshoe Siamese cat Bogart, who often sits in my lap when I write, or touches my computer keys with his paws.

TABLE OF CONTENTS

PREFACE

Writing, speaking to groups, and radio talk shows have preoccupied most of my time in 2011. I experienced a sense of restlessness unlike any I had ever experienced, a real Post Traumatic Stress Disorder. I was reliving things I had left behind 34 years ago in communist Romania. I could not understand why people did not see what was happening around us at such an accelerated pace, the "fundamental transformation" that our President had promised before his Inauguration.

The President's voting base who paid no taxes, 48 percent to be exact, seemed to be very content and even proud of his job performance. Young people were ecstatic to participate in such a momentous occasion of picking America's first black President. The rest of the population was very unhappy with the high unemployment numbers, constantly manipulated in order to bring the rate below the magical 8 percent that would help the President get re-elected. It was all about his success, not the success of our country.

It did not matter that by the fourth quarter of 2011, 13 million Americans (out of a labor force of 156 million) were unemployed, and 4 million were in the long-term unemployed category. The long-term unemployed category was defined by the Pew Fiscal Analysis Initiative as "a jobless period of a year or longer." 1.1 million jobless Americans were discouraged workers who were no longer counted, as if they had vanished into thin air. These out-of-the labor force individuals were convinced that jobs did not exist and gave up looking for work. At some point in time, as they began to search for a job, the unemployment rate climbed.

Young college graduates had unemployment rates of 25 percent. According to the Pew analysts, "workers under the age of 25 represented a larger portion of the unemployed than of the total labor force."

The shovel ready jobs never materialized in spite of massive government spending. The media was more than happy to give false information on a daily basis in order to cover up the extent of the economic disaster that their President's policies caused.

Massive and dizzying changes took place in the economy, education, the military, Wall Street, big business, and Main Street. Congress lost its powers, corruption became endemic on both sides of the isle, the separation of powers disappeared, checks and balances vanished, and freedoms evaporated, the Constitution trampled and obsolete. The czars, czarinas, the White House, Non-Governmental Organizations (NGOs), United Nations ruling over us by initiatives and public-private partnerships overwhelmed the country, while the judicial system legislated our lives and our economy from the bench.

Gargantuan bailouts, TARP (Troubled Assets Relief Program), numerous stimuli, a weak dollar, double oil prices, faux green energy, global warming scams in the face of massive snows and cooling across the globe, spreading the wealth by taking from producers and giving to the slackers, and constant government handouts turned us into a welfare nation, bankrupted financially and morally by an out-of-control spending and a presidency that stoked class envy, racial hatred, greed, Occupy Wall Street malcontents, joblessness, and dependency on a socialist nanny state.

Greedy unions, the Democrat Party, and the White House encouraged, supported, and financed the Occupy Wall Street movement. Big Labor was angry over the loss of Cadillac benefits and collective bargaining in Wisconsin. Twenty-three other states chose the Right to Work instead of automatic union membership and deductions that normally enriched the coffers of the Democrat Party.

I divided my book into four categories: American Exceptionalism, Immigration, Education, and Economy.

I owe a debt of gratitude to my husband David, my "enabler," who is always my number one fan and cheerleader. He encourages me and tolerates with great kindness my lack of technology skills and patience to acquire them.

AMERICAN EXCEPTIONALISM

Where Does American Exceptionalism Come From?

I do not remember the term exceptionalism used in the seventies when I moved south. The word had been around for quite some time in political writings. Exceptionalism was self-understood. I encountered people all the time who were proud of their heritage, their history, their lilting southern accent, and Judeo-Christian values. They opened their homes and their churches to any newcomer, foreign or domestic, and welcomed them with a healthy dose of southern wit, apple pie, and fear of God.

The small conservative community was a cocoon of safety in their collective Americanism and pride. Nobody was ashamed of being American or harboring feelings of misplaced guilt that their ancestors had committed grave errors in their "imperialistic quest of the world."

The Americans I met were proud that they had liberated Europe of fascist Italy and Germany, that they had put an end to the advancement of the Japanese Empire. Slavery had been abolished, they were all Americans; people had left feelings of hurt behind them. Nobody was talking about hyphenated Americans. They shared a common language, English, in a rich, melting pot. There was no press 2 for Spanish. The divisive liberal concept of multi-culturalism had not taken root yet.

There was great pride in owning an American passport and a privilege to travel abroad representing America. Foreigners admired Americans and wished publicly to emulate their uniqueness. Many dreamed that someday, they would be able to immigrate to the land of freedom and plenty.

I was curious how the education system worked that had produced so many successful writers, engineers, doctors, artists, and architects. What were their secrets? Was it really the school system? Was it their deep faith in God? Was it the freedom, independence, vast lands, and wide-open spaces? Was it the natural resources? Was it the political system of checks and balances, limited governmental power, or a combination of all of the above?

I was in awe that so few farmers could produce so much food not just for the domestic consumption but to export to other countries and help those in dire need from catastrophic occurrences.

I admired the selfless American volunteerism of missionaries who put their lives on the line in faraway places to improve the worldly and spiritual lives of people who were seldom appreciative or thankful.

I visited the local high school to understand the concept and role of elected v. appointed superintendents. The Department of Education did not exist, it was in the works to be inaugurated a year later, in 1980. I understood principals, the counterparts of school directors in Europe. Counselor was a strange profession. Did people really need to be told what to study? Was it not obvious whether you excelled in math and science and should pursue such a field or that you were perhaps better in humanities? Why would you bus students to school when they lived less than two miles from school? Whatever happened to walking? Why feed students in school? Was that not the parents' job?

I learned slowly that the elementary or secondary education systems were not responsible for American exceptionalism. I witnessed years later a principal hold the entire student body and faculty hostage in an auditorium for eight hours awaiting the State Department of Education investigators because five graduating seniors had the audacity to prank their own dorm lobby by spray-painting poetry on the walls. It did not suffice to suspend the five and make them repay the damage as well as repaint the lobby; they had to be expelled one week before graduation, with no diplomas. I realized that zero tolerance was the hallmark of total control by communist administrators and faculty.

The National Education Association, the teachers' union, had a very powerful lobby in primary and secondary education. Their members were certainly not the brightest nor the best prepared graduates of the College of Education, but were licensed by the state to teach. Consistent low test scores on National Teacher Exams proved their lack of preparation.

I learned that Arts and Sciences graduates, who were much better prepared in their fields of study, were not allowed to teach unless they received approval from the State Department of Education in the form of teaching licenses.

I also learned after thirty years of college teaching that exceptionalism did not come from higher education either. Communist indoctrinators made up a high percentage of the faculty, particularly those who staffed the College of Education, English, Foreign Languages, Psychology, Sociology, Counseling, Social Work, Women Studies, and any other department that offered degrees in "studies of."

The first Department of Education was created in 1867, demoted in 1868 to just an office in the Department of Interior, transferred to the Federal Security Agency in 1939 and renamed the Office of Education. In 1953, the Federal Security Agency became the Department of Health, Education, and Welfare.

Jimmy Carter signed into law The Department of Education Organization Act on October 17, 1979 thus dividing The Department of Health, Education, and Welfare into the Department of Education and The Department of Health and Human Services. The Department of Education began operating on May 16, 1980 and thus began the dumbing down of American education and socialist indoctrination in the curriculum.

In case you wonder how education fared in the U.S. prior to the establishment of the Department of Education, let us consider the exceptional achievements of Americans prior to 1979: space flight, first man on the Moon, satellites deployed in space, numerous surgical and pharmaceutical breakthroughs, architectural wonders, feats of engineering, cameras, computers, cars, bridges, railroads, interstate system, tunnels through mountains, airplanes, air conditioning, modern conveniences, washing machines, life-saving medicines, devices, surgical procedures, and thousands and thousands of other inventions produced by Americans who attended schools unsupervised, regulated, or funded by the mighty Department of Education.

Republicans opposed the Department of Education since the Constitution does not mention education and thought it an illegal federal bureaucratic intrusion into local and state affairs.

Liberals thought the Department of Education Constitutional under the Commerce Clause and the funding legal under the Taxing and Spending Clause. Pretty much everything Democrats did was justified as falling under the Commerce Clause.

Conservatives saw the Department of Education as undermining states rights while libertarians saw it as giving government too much power. President Ronald Reagan promised to eliminate the department during his 1980 presidential campaign. Sadly, he did not succeed.

Although education is decentralized in the U.S. when compared to other countries, the Department of Education plays some role in determining curricula, educational standards, and policy. The bureaucracy is daunting and the budget for 2011 was $69.9 billion.

The Department collects data on U.S. schools, enforces educational laws regarding privacy and civil rights, and pretty much influences the indoctrination of public school students. Their stated mission is to prepare students for "global competitiveness through educational excellence and equal access."

Each state controls accreditation of its teachers. Worthy of mention is the controversial No Child Left Behind Act and the pitiful performance of students in math, science, and writing when compared to other developed nations as well as poor nations. It is obvious by now, to anybody who is an independent thinker that throwing more money at education does not improve the quality of it or the students' performance.

Are Americans more exceptional or less exceptional because of the existence of the Department of Education? Let us look at the student performance data after 1980. The more dollars per pupil the U.S. has spent, the worse the students performed on standardized tests or when compared with other nations. There is only one other country that spends more for education per capita than the U.S., Luxemburg, a state the size of a postage stamp.

We seem to teach now to standardized tests only, not to long-term knowledge retention, perhaps because quick results make teachers look good and bring in funding to the school. Do teachers care if the students cannot remember much after the test? Some actually do and I was privileged to work with a few who were devoted to their profession beyond the call of duty. Our contracts were not union contracts. We were employees at will. We waited every year anxiously of the news whether we had a contract or not. We did not feel entitled to employment unless we performed well. Employment was based on our merit.

The 1995 Third International Mathematics and Science Study (TIMSS) of half a million students in 41 developed countries found that American fourth graders performed poorly, eighth graders worse, and twelfth graders were unable to compete. Grade 4 scored in the middle, grade 8 scored in the bottom third, and grade 12 scored last.

Curricula, teachers, and the textbooks were to blame. The curricula were too dumbed-down with basic arithmetic. Teachers did not have enough mathematics and science in college, their education was focused on social engineering instead of subject areas. Textbooks were also dumbed down, teaching how to use the math as opposed to how to do the math.

How then did Americans become exceptional in their 235-year history? Was it their entrepreneurship and the Wild West mentality that can conquer any adversity? Was it their work ethic and pride in a job well done? Was it their generosity and compassion to their fellow man? Was it their excellence in sports? Was it their volunteerism? Was it devotion to God and country? Was it their willingness to sacrifice in war, in a foreign land, for the cause of freedom? Was it their ability to teach themselves? Was it their independence and freedom to think and create individually?

The American exceptionalism did not come from the liberal academics who have indoctrinated their pupils for the last forty years into the utopia of socialism and the nanny state.

Young people demand more and more from their country and feel entitled to basic needs that people used to get through hard work. Now they claim, it is their right. Everything that Americans used to earn for themselves is now expected from the federal government, a lazy cradle to grave existence, following the failed European model.

Education has diminished as exemplified by test scores and by students who hold diplomas and cannot read and write proficiently. Teachers are no longer the role models of moral compass and knowledge. The lack of ethics and moral compass were on full display in 2011 among the teachers on strike and doctors in Wisconsin, and among the 14 fleeing Democrat lawmakers who chose to run and hide in Illinois instead of doing their jobs they were elected to do in Wisconsin. Never before had we witnessed former role models lie, cheat, and steal. They did not represent American exceptionalism and honor; they represented cowardice and deceit, a blight on America's collective history.

It saddens me that, for the past four years, the President has apologized for our American exceptionalism as if it was a character flaw and somehow shameful.

I am very proud of who we are as a nation. I would like to think that the American pioneer uniqueness of spirit, selfless generosity and sacrifice, the envy of the world, still exists today in the United States of America.

Who We Are As A Nation

America used to mean something. The Statue of Liberty represented independence, what it meant collectively to be an American. There was a reason why millions risked life and limb to come to our shores. We were a nation of immigrants with a strong work ethic. America was built on hard work, sweat, self-determination, and freedom. We were free and we were proud to be Americans.

We are not who liberals decide us to be. We are not children who need to be told by the government how to live and to be shameful and apologetic about our American exceptionalism. We are patriots who love our country because we feel so in our hearts, because we are free. We are not children who have to stay in their parents' homes until the age of 26, finding ourselves, because some misguided elected official says we should be on welfare and free healthcare.

If we give to the less fortunate, it is because we want to give, not because the president thinks that we must spread the wealth and re-distribute it according to some grand, global scheme, punishing us for our "evil capitalist" ways. Most middle class Americans have worked hard for what they have, why should they find themselves broke when nearing retirement because progressives think that "social justice" must be implemented.

Our Constitution guards and protects private property. Who are United Nations and all its progressive affiliates to tell us that private property is the root of discrimination and must thus be abolished, stolen, and re-distributed to the poor of the world? The Bible says, "Thou shall not steal."

Who made progressives the arbiters of the American Dream? What if we do not want to live a simpler life and we like our lives just the way they are, consumerism and all, good or bad? Are they going to come and force us to change to their vision of what living should be? Our consumerism keeps millions of Chinese and Americans financially secure and employed.

Not all Americans have personal possessions to sell, savings to rely on, or rich relatives, we have to work. We cannot take time off to find ourselves in a foreign land, on a mountain peak, an African village, or on the open sea. I personally like what I do. When you really like what you do, you do it free. Moreover, I do not want someone else telling me what I like.

Flooding our country with billions of dollars in stimulus spending or dollars not backed by goods and services is not going to solve our problem. It will cause further debt and inflation. There is something wrong with what we teach our children. We no longer teach them to be self-sufficient, to seize the opportunity, "Carpe Diem," we teach them to expect cradle to grave mentality, dependence on the nanny state because it is a "right" and an "entitlement."

Free healthcare is not a right. Healthcare is a service like any other service that we must pay for. Who says that a doctor who spent 12 years in college to become a doctor and half a million dollars in tuition fees and books suddenly owes you free care? Are you going to clean his house, mow his lawn, do his laundry, and fix his computers free of charge?

The American culture is not about non-producers living off the producers. This is not who we are. Maybe it is what lefties want us to be, pining for European lifestyles that are failing left and right, no pun intended. We were somebody when we believed in free market capitalism. We thrived when we believed in the American spirit, in individuality, in freedom of choice, of religion, of speech. We are in such disarray; we are no longer that nation. We have to get our public policy in order so we can be that nation again. We have to get rid of all corrupt politicians on both sides.

The status quo is no longer an option. It has demoralized the country because we no longer see a solution to the myriad of problems that are being created at a very fast pace every day. We are a divided population in crisis right now, saddled by immense debt. We have to go back to the values that made this country great. There is no other way to extricate ourselves from this quandary. Furthermore, we do not want a one-world government that the ruling elites are pushing. Our Constitution and our legal system are incompatible with Sharia Law. We have to stop its spread in this country. We cannot have two legal system in America, it is not who we are.

Health insurance is a moral hazard not a right. You choose to purchase it and use it a lot or you choose to take your chances that you will not get sick and save your money for other emergencies. Nothing is free, there is an opportunity cost associated with any activity. Somebody has to produce housing, healthcare, education, food, otherwise it does not exist.

The American culture was not steeped on spending trillions more dollars than we actually take in taxes. Turning one group of society against another is not the American culture that our fore fathers built. Turning people against the rich is hatred and class division pure and simple; it is not a logical solution to the out-of-control spending.

The rich pay plenty of taxes and so does the middle class. It is true that the bottom 47 percent of income earners pays no federal and state taxes. The problem is that the government is spending us shamelessly into oblivion with each year's base line budgeting and they do not seem to want to stop in spite of citizens' protests.

We also pay lavishly for illegal aliens and their children, it must stop, and their home countries must care of them. We should give them emergency care, but the rest is up to their countries. Their anchor babies should not be our responsibility.

If we confiscated everybody's wealth and income in the nation, it will offset spending and national debt ($14 trillion) for about a year. What will we do after that? Who is going to create jobs and thus a national income? Do we revert to a hunter-gatherer society?

A Walk Through History

The Potomac River shines through the barren trees. The marina nearby is empty although the weather is balmy for late November. I can hear the laughter of children playing at the water's edge. I feel lucky and privileged to walk on Lee's historical trail in Leesylavania Woods, Virginia.

A white marble obelisk in the middle of a roundabout draws my attention. It is dedicated to Henry Lee III, "Light Horse Harry," 1756-1818, whose accomplishments are inscribed on the simple monument:

- Cavalry Commander 1776-1781
- Congressional Medal 1779
- Member Continental Congress 1786-1788
- Governor of Virginia 1791-1794
- Member U.S. Congress 1799-1801
- Father of General Robert E. Lee

Henry Lee III is buried in Lexington, Virginia but Henry Lee II and his wife Lucy are resting in the Lee and Fairfax family cemetery – a long trek to the tombs on a small ridge of the peninsula overlooking the Occoquan Bay. The headstones had long disappeared, replaced by a bronze plaque.

A solitary artillery piece "defends" a bluff - a 32 pounder similar to those used by the Confederate Army under the command of General Robert E. Lee who ordered the Blockade of the Potomac River from October 1861 to March 1862.

Through small openings in the thick and dormant vegetation, the bay glitters in the afternoon sun. If I close my eyes, I can imagine Captain John Smith exploring and mapping the Potomac in the summer of 1608.

I am standing on the village "Niobsco" ("at the point of the rock") landmark where friendly Doeg tribes lived. The hostile Petomec Indians made their villages downriver. Algonquian Indians inhabited the Virginia Waterways. There must be ample archeological evidence of

Indian habitation buried beneath my feet because metal detectors are forbidden.

There are a few boats out on the water in the lazy afternoon sun. I can picture the barges in 1872 loading up schooners with firewood, lumber, livestock, fruit, hay, and slate on their way to Washington. There is a pier going out into the bay. Half way down, a red plaque indicates the Maryland line. I am no longer in Virginia's maritime territory, I am in Maryland.

As I come up a gentle hill, a lone fireplace with a chimneystack marks the former home of John W. Fairfax, a colonel in the Confederate Army. His farm had a main barn built into the side of the hill. All that is left of the barn are some sandstone foundation blocks, cut from the cliff on Freestone Point, and covered now by green moss.

The water well's brick walls are still visible. It would be quite a hike to carry water up these hills. Who carried it before the well was dug up? How did they bring supplies up from the river's edge? For many years, the Leesylvania Plantation produced tobacco but in the summer of 1859, food was more important: rich fields of corn, wheat, rye, and oats swayed in the wind.

Henry Lee II had purchased the newly cleared fields of the peninsula in September 1754 to produce tobacco, a very sought after crop during those times in England. His new bride, Lucy, had named the area, "Leesylvania," Lee's Woods.

Lucy Grimes Lee and Henry Lee II are buried in the cemetery on a grassy knoll, now covered with a carpet of dry leaves. The grave markers have been removed long time ago. The state park encircled their remains with a black metal fence and a bronze plaque.

I wonder what Henry Lee II and his famous son, "Light Horse Harry," would say if they knew that a naturalized citizen like me, from a former communist country, appreciates the country they and their descendants have built through much sacrifice and bloodshed, much more than most natural-born Americans. Would they approve and would they be proud of the direction that our country is taking?

Lucy, the daughter of a wealthy plantation owner, once rejected the attentions of a shy suitor, George Washington. His plantation, a state of the art farm for its time, is located not far away at Mount Vernon.

Lucy and Henry Lee II had been married for 34 years and produced eight children. Their famous son is "Light Horse Harry." Henry Lee II served in public office in Prince William County and in Virginia for many years.

Captain Henry Fairfax purchased nearly two thousand acres of Leesylvania in 1825 from Alfred Lee, the grandson of Henry Lee II. The captain brought his wife to a home built in 1803, 500 yards from the original Lee home. He and his wife raised seven children here from 1825 until their deaths in 1847. Both are buried in the same cemetery on the grassy knoll with Lucy Grimes Lee.

Captain Fairfax's descendants rebuilt the original home and inhabited the place until 1908 when it burned to the ground. As I walk past his former homestead, a huge white oak (Quercus Alba), marked as Prince William County's Bicentennial Tree, blocks the trail. A soft and very thick carpet of dead leaves is evidence that the oak is very much alive. If it could only talk, the stories would fill up volumes!

A peaceful silence surrounds my crunching steps as I carefully watch the thick roots like veins pulsing with green blood, ready to trip me as the hills become steeper. A soft wind whispers through the barren branches. They arch upwards, reaching for the clear blue sky.

Lucy's former garden left behind many species of plants and trees such as the Paw Paw, the American Beech (Fagus Grandifolia), flowering dogwood (Cornus Florida), and the white oak (Quercus Alba). I was hoping to find traces of the tobacco plants.

The small triangular nuts of the beech tree were eaten whole, ground into flour, pressed for oil, or roasted to make ersatz "coffee." The wood of the white oak made good wine barrels. The dogwood was extremely shock resistant and thus used to make tool handles and mallet heads.

As I reach the top of a very steep hill, there seems to be the end of the road. A deep valley below bears witness to the former railroad tracks that were cut into the hill and used from 1872-1925.

The valley was excavated shortly after the Civil War. The rail ran between Washington, D.C. and Richmond, Virginia, a symbol of a reunited nation. It was built by Alexandria and Fredericksburg Railroad.

Landslides and train derailments plagued the area and often temporary and rigged repairs were made to accommodate passing trains. P.T. Barnum and his circus, on the way to Fredericksburg, Virginia, remarked, "he had been all over the United States, but this was the first railroad he had ever seen tied to a tree."

The plant and animal life seemed to have changed little since Captain John Smith said in his 1627 book, *A General History of Virginia*, "Virginia doth afford many excellent vegetable and living creatures, yet grass there is little or none, but what groweth in low marshes; for all the country is overgrown with trees… The wood that is most common is oak and walnut…There is also some elm, some black walnut trees and ash."

I ponder this quote as I marvel at the thickness of woods everywhere. I am not sure, I could walk this trail when everything is green and overgrown. I would definitely get lost and the terrain would be less accessible. It certainly is not true what environmentalists claim that European pilgrims deforested Virginia in their path and ruined the fishing stock by overfishing, committing "biological imperialism."

The Potomac is still teeming with fish - waterfowl do not seem to starve. Beavers have built dams along the river. Deer, foxes, rabbits, birds of prey, egrets, Canadian geese, ducks, turtles and other species, too many to name, are abundant. Fishing is prohibited but it does not stop a few die-hard anglers.

Nature has a way of coming back, renewing itself in the most unusual places. A long ago fallen and rotting trunk is sprouting green saplings all over. An uprooted tree is still alive, feeding itself in a horizontal position from the rich soil beneath.

I was humbled today to walk in the footsteps of history of such a beautiful country. I am proud and lucky to be an American, to live so close to the beginnings of our exceptional nation. Jamestown, Mount Vernon, Fredericksburg, Williamsburg, and Monticello are only a short drive away.

People from all over the world had worked extremely hard to overcome so many difficulties in America. In the end, despite the Civil War, they were united by one culture, one history, one language, love of God, and a fierce desire for freedom and independence from oppression.

The Heartbreak of the Last Shuttle Flight

The last shuttle flight took off majestically with a plume of fire, disappearing into the clouds within forty seconds into its last man-made exploration, perhaps a fitting metaphor for its meteoric rise and fall. The smaller than usual crew consisted of three men and a woman, a precautionary move in case technical difficulties stranded them in space. It would cost the United States $63 million for each astronaut that the Russian Soyuz would return to earth. We have become mere passengers, taking a back seat to Russia's leading role and military ambitions in cosmos.

It is a sad end to a program spanning decades of space exploration that has improved the quality of life for billions of citizens. Many inventions that civilization takes for granted are the result of NASA engineers and their quest for perfection.

NASA excelled in Earth Science, Planetary Science, Astrophysics, and Heliophysics. It encompassed Aeronautics Research, Space Technology, Space Exploration, Space Education, and Space Operations.

According to Erik Sterner, NASA's former associate deputy administrator for policy and planning, NASA's budget for 2011 was roughly $18.5 billion, 0.5 percent of a $3.7 trillion federal budget, as much as Americans spent on pet food in 2010. "At the height of the Apollo program, NASA consumed more than 4 percent of the federal budget. In the 1960s, that was a lot of money. Today, it's a rounding error."

Since 1976, NASA accumulated a list of every commercialized technology and product linked to its research such as improved pacemakers, exercise machines, satellite radio and filed 63,000 patents. Some discoveries have not yet shown all implications for science and humanity: a solar system 127 light years away, solar flares, alien life on Saturn's moon Titan, detailed pictures of earth, and frozen water on the moon.

I found many inventions that NASA pioneered in conjunction with its many contractors. To protect the infrared antennae of heat seeking missile trackers, a new use was discovered for the translucent polycrystalline aluminum, invisible braces.

NASA needed a special coating to protect space equipment, especially astronaut helmet visors, from dirt and particles found in space. Foster Grant delivered scratch resistant lenses.

"The open cell polyurethane-silicon plastic was created for use in NASA aircraft seats to lessen impact during landings. The plastic has a unique property that allows it to evenly distribute the weight and pressure on top of it, which provides shock absorbency. Even after being compressed to 10 percent of its size, the memory foam will return to its original shape." Memory foam is now used in prosthetic limbs, by bed manufacturers, and by hospitals to ease pain and reduce bedsores.

NASA's Jet Propulsion Lab invented an infrared sensor that serves as a thermometer. Aural thermometers with these infrared sensors take temperature instantly by measuring the amount of energy the eardrum gives off into the ear canal.

Neil Armstrong's famous moon boots provided inspiration for Avia and Kangaroos tennis shoes to include the technology and the materials that absorb shock.

Before humans were sent into space, NASA built satellites that could communicate with people on the ground. Over 200 communication satellites orbit the globe each day. These satellites send and receive messages that allow us to call our friends anywhere in the world and use our wireless devices. NASA monitors the locations and health of many of these satellites.

NASA did not develop Tang, as it is widely believed. General Mills invented it in 1957. It was attributed to NASA because it was one of the foods that could be easily carried to and used in space.

In the 1970s, the designed space station Skylab needed a reliable smoke detector that would not give faulty readings, thus the adjustable smoke detector was invented.

NASA's Langley Research Center experimented in the 1960s with safety grooving as a way to improve safety to aircraft taking off on wet runways. Today it is used around swimming pools, pedestrian crosswalks, animal pens, and highways. Road accidents have decreased by 85 percent as result of safety grooving.

In preparation for the Apollo missions in the 1960s, NASA and

Black & Decker developed cordless tools, lightweight, compact, and powerful, with a battery that would last longer in space with a magnet-motor drill.

Water filtration existed since early 1950s, but NASA introduced the tiny black flecks, apart from the charcoal chunks. These tiny black flecks are specially activated with silver ions that neutralize pathogens in water, killing bacteria and preventing further growth.

Virgin Galactic is trying to provide space transportation but most of NASA's missions are not commercially possible to replicate because there is no consumer demand for robotic missions to Mars, Hubble Space Telescopes, and Alpha Magnetic Spectrometers. Private investment is usually prompted by demand.

Fifty years passed since President Kennedy's speech, which announced that man would be sent to the moon. I still remember the moon landing and the controversy surrounding it. There are still Americans today who claim that the whole affair was staged and we never planted the American flag on the lunar landscape.

NASA was founded in 1958, a year after Sputnik was placed into orbit. President Eisenhower wanted a peaceful mission into space unlike the Russians who wanted to display their military power. President Kennedy wanted to win. President Reagan said, at the start of the space station program in 1984, "We are first; we are the best; and we are so because we are free." We never wanted to colonize space - that was Hollywood's fantasy.

NASA set the pace and was the world leader in space exploration. We are no longer number one. Nine other countries have placed payloads into orbit, including India, China, Iran, and Israel. Fifty or more nations design, deploy, own, or operate satellites in space such as China, Brazil, and Japan. China and Japan mapped the moon. India launched a robotic moon mission in 2008 in co-operation with Russia. Will we ever go to the moon again? Will we go to Mars as the president desires? Does he even realize it takes 288 days to get there?

The Universal Man described as "ten men in one," Leonardo da Vinci (1452-1519), had envisioned flight beyond the myth of Daedalus and Icarus with their waxed wings which melted in the sun. Leonardo from the little town of Vinci left behind a detailed notebook with plans for flying machines, a parachute, a helicopter, a diving suit, a military tank, and a split-level city.

And here we are today, at a fork in the road, our manned space exploration dreams killed with the ignorant stroke of an executive order pen.

Oath of Office

We never give it a thought when we sign our names to a 78-page document agreeing to whatever terms and conditions the document entails. We are in a hurry to use the new game, application, or program that our computers and electronic gadgets download.

If we are so casual and eager to sign a document that we have no idea what it says nor do we care or understand its ramifications, I wonder, how valuable is the oath of office that public employees must swear in order to uphold the rules, duties, and responsibilities implied therein?

Do judges uphold the law impartially as they swore to do, or do they interpret each case before the court to suit their political views, their activism, or the administration of the moment?

Do police officers serve and protect everyone equally and take bullets in the line of duty for total strangers because they have sworn an oath to defend all citizens from harm?

Do soldiers swear allegiance to the Constitution, knowing that they place their lives in harm's way for their country, for their fellow Americans who sometimes disrespect what they do and deride their patriotism?

Do men and women in uniform know and understand that they might give their lives for the indolent and malcontent squatters who claim that the rich owe them a living from cradle to grave?

Would all soldiers defend the Constitution if called upon to do so, or would they follow orders contrary to their oath?

Should we weep in outrage that Old Glory, our cherished flag, the last cloth that drapes returning coffins from the battlefield, is burned and trampled by other Americans who do not care about the sacrifice, altruism, and exceptionalism of their fellow American volunteer soldiers?

Many generations of Americans gave their lives for our freedom to speak freely and assemble anywhere they want peacefully. They swore an oath and kept it. They had honor.

Did they die so that malcontents can burn the flag, demand the wealth of the rich in doped-up frenzy, infringe on our rights to enjoy a park free of litter, free of bums urinating and defecating in public, free of paid youth without a compass who direct their supposed anger to the wrong segment of society? The very people who destroyed their ability to find a job are the ones stoking hatred and paying them to protest the rest of us who are job creators and engines of economic growth.

Did TSA agents remember the oath they had signed and sworn to protect Americans from potential terrorism? They must have forgotten, otherwise they would not be groping and molesting innocent Americans, the elderly, the handicapped, and small children, in the misplaced eagerness to accomplish the ill-advised marching orders.

Have Congressmen forgotten that they had sworn an oath to protect and serve the interests of the American people, that they truly are civil servants to the Republic? They certainly behave as omnipotent masters not servants to the people. The laws they pass are so damaging and counterproductive to the interests of "we the people" that their oath has become meaningless and worthless.

Have teachers forgotten that their duty is to disseminate the truth objectively, free of hatred, envy, personal ideology, religious creed, union and party affiliation bias? Have they forgotten their very important moral responsibility to shape future Americans in our Founding Fathers' wise vision?

Will doctors violate the Hippocratic Oath in order to deliver "socially just" and rationed medical care according to the new and improved Obama healthcare law? Will they provide lesser care to the detriment of the patients in order to fulfill the law's requirements?

Will firefighters and police officers be unable to respond to the citizens' needs as quickly and as often, because Congress failed to pass President Obama's new and generous for unions jobs bill, or will they follow their oath?

When we sign our names on a document, a promissory note, a contract, a bank check, an **oath of office,** we put our honor on the line and agree to deliver on that promise.

Honor is the last bastion of our humanity, of our freedom. Honor defines who we are. As Publilius Syrus said, "What is left when honor is lost?" Without honor, we are nothing, and we have nothing.

Demonizing America's Silent Conservative Majority from Canada

On May Day, the international holiday of communists, the *Washington Post* editorial used Jonathan Kay's book, "Among the Truthers: A Journey through America's Growing Conspiracist Underground," to besmirch and demonize the silent conservative majority of America. The left's constant ideological wars against the taxpaying middle class and the job creators continue.

Jonathan Kay, the managing editor of *Canada's National Post,* claims that he has interviewed hundreds of conspiracy theorists in the past three years. He theorizes that they have a "twisted relationship with reality" and explains it through the taxonomy of "true fake believers."

The first group is the "apocalyptic doomsayers," those who fantasize about good vs. evil. The most prominent person Kay picks to exemplify this category is Joseph Farah and his popular WorldNet Daily website as an example. The entire monolithic readership, in Kay's opinion, "thinks conservative American values must battle an Islamist, Afrocentric, socialist president bent on destroying the country."

I am looking at the economic destruction around me, the loss of homes, high inflation, high unemployment, high gas prices, schizophrenic foreign policies, excessive adulation of Islam, constant apologies to the world, endless cash for United Nations third world dictatorship, the Arab Spring which looks more like the Arab Winter, moratoriums on oil drilling, wasteful spending, TARP, stimulus 1, stimulus 2, confiscation of GM and Chrysler bondholder assets and redistribution to American unions and Fiat, bailouts for Fannie Mae and Freddie Mac, school loan Fed takeover, debasing the dollar, cash for clunkers, cash for caulkers, driving up the price of coal on purpose, czars, global warming hoax, and I wonder, is this destruction on purpose or accidental due to incompetence? It is not that our national debt looms larger than it has ever been in the entire U.S. history; it is that we are "apocalyptic doomsayers."

"Failed Historians" is the second group of the American "fringe," exemplified in Kay's opinion by the extreme example of the Holocaust Denier fascinated by Nazism. I recall that Tea Party groups were called Nazis ad nauseam by various members of the current administration with no apology or condemnation for hate speech.

I also recall the "progressives" branding President Bush and his administration Nazis for eight years straight. Many violent student protests burned Bush's Nazi-like effigy, causing property damage in the process, with no commentary from the state-controlled media about the appropriateness of such acts, and maintenance of respect and decorum.

Kay's third category of conspiracy theorists is the "Mentally Unbalanced." I do not know how many mentally ill he has interviewed or what qualifies him as a psychiatrist and diagnostician. It is an offensive attempt to categorize and malign the conservative movement as composed of mentally ill just because they disagree with the ideology of the left. It is reminiscent of the Soviet era when dissenters were taken to mental hospitals and treated in large wards with hard-core drugs in order to change their anti-communistic behavior and ultimately turn them into pliant drones who could no longer think for themselves.

The fourth category of the "paranoid fringe" is the "Midlife Crisis Case." Apparently Kay met many conspiracy theorists who were fat 40-50 year old men; they joined the ranks because of failed lives and disappointing relationships. This is interesting because I did see thousands and thousands of families and couples at rallies that were unhappy with the government spending, not with their families or unfulfilled careers. They were law-abiding citizens who believed in God, loved their country deeply, and waved American flags. I also saw the far-left Code Pink in various states of undress, wearing loony, ridiculous costumes, supporting causes that were and are always opposite of American mainstream values.

Finally, yet importantly, are the "Fakers." Kay theorizes that Donald Trump is the ultimate "birther" and "faker" who used his platform to galvanize the "Republican Party's Obama-phobic base," and to boost his empire holdings while increasing the ratings for the "Apprentice." His explanation for Donald's fakery is the statement made by Washington Post that Trump has donated more money to Democrats than to Republicans. This begs the question, how are the rest of conservatives "fakers?" I guess this category must be composed of one "faker," Donald Trump.

Jonathan Kay concludes that not all theorists are "unhinged, bug-eyed loners." Some Americans who come in "respectable guises" still do not believe that President Obama was born in the United States although he released his long-form birth certificate. Respectable citizens comprise the rest of the conspiracy theorists. Even Americans with money are not sheltered from a "twisted relationship with reality," says Jonathan Kay. Mr. Kay seems to have an interesting but distorted take on reality.

Constitution Day Celebration

You are Americans by the grace of God. You were lucky to be born in the land of the free and the brave. Many foreigners risk their lives and fortunes to come here, while leaving behind everything they love and hold dear in order to be free. I am such a foreigner, I came from communist Romania in 1978.

I am a proud American by choice. Thirty-four years ago, my father gave up his only child when he signed the legal permission for my journey to America, knowing that he may never see me again. He understood very well that I wanted to be free and to develop my fullest potential without crushing government control. I wanted the opportunity to pursue my dreams, to break away from the poverty of the communist "proletariat." We all knew that a better life and future waited in America if I only worked hard. I could not progress and maintain a conscience under the oppression of a communist dictatorship.

I have just returned from a visit to Romania. In the 25 years since my last visit, Romania has changed so much that it is now in some ways more capitalist and freer than we are. Twenty-five years ago, the boot of communism was still pressing heavily on the neck of the collective population. It was sad and depressing to watch the suffering, the political, economic, and religious persecution of my family and of citizens in general. I could not stand to witness it and I stopped visiting.

The communists were overthrown in December 1989 through a bloody revolution. They were overwhelmingly rejected from power but sadly not gone; they were still there in the shadows, re-emerging now like a malignant cancer. I visited their Social Democrat and European Socialist Party headquarters in my home town. They are promising the same hollow, tired "hope and change" utopia.

The elderly, used to the nanny state, whose pensions were recently cut due to bureaucratic mismanagement, waste, and corruption are being told that their lives would be better under communism because they would be given a free loaf of bread, a dingy and dilapidated one-bedroom subsidized apartment, and an aspirin when disease struck. It was disheartening to watch how short people's memory is. Young people entertain romanticized versions of socialism and communism. I have not forgotten the miserable life I lived under communism.

It was empowering to see my first cousin build a very successful manufacturing company through hard work and entrepreneurship. It took him 15 years of twelve-hour workdays but he succeeded because the new capitalist system that replaced the communist one removed initially all restrictions placed on political, religious, and economic freedoms of its citizens. For the first time since 1990, he was able to travel and work abroad, unencumbered by the existence of a relative in the "evil" capitalist U.S.

I still remember his meager one room city rental under communism with his wife and infant daughter. Their urban residence was denied because social engineering under communism required domicile in the place of birth. Mobility was restricted unless the Communist Party allowed it and permission was granted. They fought for years unsuccessfully to change their status from rural to urban. He had dreams and plans that were forbidden by the ruling regime. He is now a benefactor to many churches that are built not just in his village but all over the country. By the last count, over 6,000 new churches were dedicated and blessed since the fall of communism.

I visited my father's grave and I renewed my promise that he did not die in vain at the hands of communists. I vowed that I will return more resolute to fight those who wish us harm, who want to fundamentally transform our society into their utopian image of an egalitarian nation in which everybody is equally poor, equally miserable, equally beholden and dependent on an omnipotent nanny government who wants to control every aspect of our lives.

I am happy to return to the shining city on the hill with trepidation in my heart. America is now my country and my home. America needs our help to save it and preserve it the way our founding fathers had intended 225 years ago when they drafted the perfect document, our Constitution.

The U.S. Constitution, handwritten by Jacob Shallus, was adopted on September 17, 1787. It is the second oldest written constitution still in use by any nation (after the 1600 statutes of San Marino). It has been amended 27 times, last time ratified on May 7, 1992.

The first ten amendments are known as the Bill of Rights.

By comparison, the 2010 Romanian Constitution has 156 articles and has been modified at least a dozen times according to the type of governance in power, monarchy, socialist republic, communism, and republic.

Times are uncertain and scary. We must not remain silent; we must fight back the shredding of our Constitution and the trampling of our legal system, of our checks and balances. We must restore America to its greatness.

We must never be ashamed to be Americans. We are an exceptional nation and our exceptionalism comes from our ethical, moral, and religious values that founded this country. The pioneer spirit for good is still alive in every one of us.

Do not take freedoms for granted! Freedom is not free, millions of faceless Americans have died to preserve it so that I may write today, so that I can return to my beloved adopted country and still have a voice in our collective future.

Millions of Americans have died and are still dying today to free other peoples from oppression. Our heroes are resting at Arlington National Cemetery, some in faraway countries, their courage and sacrifice never forgotten. They are in our hearts and prayers.

It means something to be an American who comes to the aid of so many, no questions asked, with food, medicine, disaster relief, re-building, and giving hope to so many. When Americans come to a part of the world, they are a beacon of salvation and of hope.

The beacon of hope is flickering. I wonder every day what freedoms have we lost while we were sleeping. If we keep silent, we resign to a fate of losing our Constitutional Republic to an ideology of phony "hope and change" that nobody understood initially but it is now abundantly clear. Do we want change for the sake of change, change to buy more votes, more power, more influence? Do we want change that causes economic disasters and enslaves us? The answer is a resounding no. We want freedom and the all-encompassing perfect Constitution to protect it.

Islam's Scant Contribution to America

The Alexandrian Library in Cairo was accidentally set on fire during Julius Caesar's brief campaign in Egypt in 48 B.C. One of the scholars who worked at the Alexandrian Library was a woman named Hypatia, born in 370 A.D., the daughter of the mathematician Theon of Alexandria. She instructed students on Plato, Aristotle, Pythagoras, and other Greek philosophers. She was regarded as a pagan. A Christian mob led by monks, possibly carrying out the wishes of Bishop Cyril of Alexandria who hated paganism, caused a riot during which she was dragged from her chariot, stripped, and flayed alive with clam shells.

Alexandria was the center of learning during the third century A.D. and a center of Christian worship. It appears that in 391 A.D., a mob destroyed the pagan temple of the Egyptian god Serapis, the Serapeum, and with it part of the Alexandrian Library, which was housed in the building.

Scholars claim that part of the library survived. The final destruction was caused by Arab invaders in 646 A.D. They destroyed all books that did not conform to the teachings of Islam. It is said that the scrolls from the Alexandrian Library were burned for months in the public baths as fuel to heat the water. Centuries old wisdom went up in smoke to bathe Islam.

I became intrigued by claims made by our administration that Islam has contributed immensely to our Judeo-Christian culture in America and I set out to find evidence of such contribution.

The first scientist I found was "mad" Alhazen of Cairo, born in Iraq in 965 A.D. He allegedly mastered mathematics, philosophy, physics, and medicine knowledge of that time by the age of 30. He drew the attention of the Caliph of Egypt, Al-Hakim who invited him to Cairo.

Alhazen advised the Caliph to dam the Nile at the logical place, the gorge of Aswan. The tools of that time made it impossible to dam the river. The Caliph executed men who disappointed his high expectations but Alhazen admitted failure, telling the king that he was not responsible since he was out of his mind. Islamic law forbade the killing of madmen.

The cyclical flooding of the river Nile in summer and drought in spring was finally controlled in 1971 when a large dam was built at Aswan, Egypt, supposedly the exact point proposed by Alhazen.

Alhazen found that, when an object placed in a dark room irradiated by light passing through a tiny hole, an inverted image of that object would appear, the principle of photography. Such claim has no manuscripted evidence.

One hundred years after Mohammed's death in 632, his followers occupied an area stretching from India to Spain. The Arabs absorbed from their subjects, the Greeks, Jews, Persians, and Christian Syrians everything from architecture to Greek philosophy. It is claimed that translations of ancient philosophers and scientists were disseminated and studied in Islamic schools. Muslim Spain is said to have reintroduced Aristotle to Christian Europe through the Cordoba Library that held 600,000 volumes. This behavior seemed contradictory since Arabs burned Alexandria Library's remaining scrolls in order to heat their bathhouses.

Most Muslims were accepting the ancient Greeks' interpretation of the natural world based on trust. Avicenna (980-1037) is said to have written 250 books in experimental physics and medicine. The word "algebra" derives from the Arabic word for the system, *al-djabr*, the word chemistry from *"Kehmia,"* an old name for Egypt, where chemical studies were more advanced.

It is also said that ammonia, borax, nitric acid, and sulfuric acid were identified by Muslims. The concept of zero and the decimal system is also attributed to medieval Arab mathematicians.

The Sahara Desert had been traveled by Muslim nomadic merchants who traded in gold, ivory, and salt during regular routes. In 1352, an Arab traveler from Tangier, Morocco, crossed the desert purely for the purpose of exploration. Ibn Battuta inspired the well-documented pilgrimage to Mecca of Emperor Mansa Musa, ruler of the Mande Empire of Mali (1312-1337).

Ibn Battuta made a *"hadj"* (pilgrimage) to Mecca in 1325, followed by a 24-year-long world tour which covered most of the Muslim world at the time, East Africa, India, Sri Lanka, Sumatra, and China, making a longer stop in the Maldives Islands where he became a *"qadi"* (judge) and received four wives.

Early in the eighth century, Arab and Berber armies crossed the Strait of Gibraltar from Africa and conquered most of the Iberian Peninsula. For the next six centuries, most of Spain was in the hands of the Muslims (Moors). Moorish innovations such as irrigation techniques and new crops, sugar, oranges, lemons, were said to have been brought to the continent.

Cordoba, the capital of the Muslim Andalucía, "tolerated" Christians and Jews because non-Muslims were subjected to a poll tax, the amount of which was related to income and could be paid in installments. Modern scholars claim that the poll tax was such a great source of revenue for the Moors, that they discouraged conversion to Islam. As long as non-Muslim subjects did not insult their Prophet or the tenets of Islam, Christian and Jews could run their own religious affairs. Which begs the question, if Muslims were so tolerant, why did the Christians rebel and re-claim their territory in 1492?

Sultans, viziers, and caliphs were important political men to the Muslim world, although to western ears they seem to be characters in "1,000 Arabian Nights" stories. A *caliph* was the highest title and considered the successor to Muhammad and therefore the spiritual head of all Islam, holding both religious and political power. *Sultans* were like kings and emperors, supreme temporal rulers in a territory with no spiritual power over the clergy. A *vizier* was a monarch's chief of staff, appointed by sultans or caliphs. *Emirs* were commanders in both military and civil sense. They were de facto generals or colonels of Islamic armies or even governors of a monarch's territory.

The President said that Islam "carried the light of learning through so many centuries, paving the way for Europe's Renaissance and Enlightenment," and praised "innovation in Muslim communities that developed the order of algebra; our magnetic compass and tools of navigation; our mastery of pens and printing; our understanding of how disease spreads and how it can be healed." I wonder if the president ever heard of the German Johannes Gutenberg, the inventor of the printing press in 1450.

The Roman Marcus Terentius Varro made references to microbes when he warned against locating a homestead near swamps "because there are bred certain minute creatures which cannot be seen by the eyes, which float in the air and enter the body through the mouth and nose and there cause serious diseases."

Robert Spencer wrote, "The idea that Islamic culture was once a beacon of learning and enlightenment is a commonly held myth. In fact, much of this has been exaggerated, often for quite transparent apologetic motives."

The exaggerated role of Islam is a revisionist attempt to inflate the Arab culture. As my very wise grandmother would say, a few flowers of wisdom do not constitute an enlightened and sunny spring.

Since When are Independence Day Parades Right Wing?

Who can object to a patriotic parade but a progressive from Harvard who finds somehow that a 4th of July parade is a political stunt aimed at garnering new converts to the Republican Party?

A recent Harvard Kennedy School of Government study published its three key findings:

- Attendees to the July 4th parades before the age of 18 are likely to identify as Republicans by a "whopping" 2 percent
- People watching parades are "likely" to vote as Republicans by another "whopping" 4 percent
- Parade "revelers" will "likely" make a contribution of 3 percent to Republicans

Since when is patriotism, joy, and pride of being American, of celebrating 235 years of history, accomplishments, and fantastic success right-wing and for sale? It is if you are a "progressive" who is anti-American and tries to tarnish American values and symbols under the pseudo-scientific guise of research for research's sake by taking cheap shots at the GOP and freedom loving Americans.

Paul Bedard, the author of the article, recommends, "Democratic political candidates can skip this weekend's July 4th parades." Celebrations are going to boost GOP turnout on Election Day and turn children into Republicans, so why waste your time attending if you are a Democrat.

Could it be because a large majority of Americans loves their country, its history, its national anthem, its flag, and its symbolism? Could it be that Americans respect all branches of the military and the sacrifices they have made throughout its storied existence?

Could it be because Republicans are true, honorable, and devoted Americans who talk about their country with pride, shed their blood willingly and volunteer in large contingents to preserve freedom all over the world, even for those who trash and tarnish America's image with every opportunity?

Yanagizawa-Drott suggests that "if people are looking for a super-patriotic July 4, should head to Republican towns. Republican adults celebrate Fourth of July more intensely." Did these people spend serious time creating this worthless report? It is shameless to transform love and devotion to our country into a political tool.

I am absolutely incensed that political and class warfare are spreading more malignancy to every aspect of American life, egged on by our administration who promotes separation, hatred, class envy, group envy, warfare, and strife. Can we not celebrate the birth of our wonderful Republic, of our Independence Day, without judgmental calls from the left?

July 4 should be an opportunity to revel in being American, in being free from oppression, free to speak, free to worship the church of your choice, free to congregate, free to be yourself, free to move to the town and state of your choice. It is about coming together as a nation, willingly, not because a centralized government forces us to come out and march in odious communistic parades with the dear leader watching from a platform, surrounded by ruling oligarchs, while the forced- to-be adoring crowds cheer on cue or else.

Our country's Independence Day is not about votes and political partisanship, as progressives try to portray it, it is about American pride, something liberals lack most definitely.

This naturalized American citizen by choice is proud to live in the world's best country, to take advantage of its every opportunity to be free, to become anything I want if I work hard, without anybody with superior indignation, attitude, pseudo-science, and faux righteousness telling me what to do every step of the way.

July 4 is about fireworks, remembering the intense fights for freedom when real rockets exploded and glared in the sky in the fight for our independence from oppression and non-representation.

July 4 is about those Americans resting at Arlington National Cemetery who died to give us the freedoms that most take for granted and can be lost easily if we do not watch the enemy within and without.

July 4 is about bringing together neighbor with neighbor, celebrating this magnificent country that is the last bastion of freedom, the proverbial shining city on the hill blessed by God.

Being a Conservative

When I was a young woman, my liberal academic colleagues would ask, how I could possibly be a conservative since I was a teacher, a single mother of two, and quite poor, way below the government-established poverty line.

I shrugged my shoulders and ignored the question every time. I knew I could not sway their basic core beliefs, no matter what I said. How could they understand what it was like living under a tyrannical Marxist government? Even people on welfare in this country, who consider themselves poor and whine about economic inequality, the greedy rich, and the "evil capitalism," live better than 99.9 percent of people on the planet.

The current young and very liberal generations accuse their elders of not wanting change and not understanding the need to protect the environment at all costs. As a conservative, I embrace change that is meaningful, not change that would "fundamentally transform" who we are. I do not wish to become beholden to government for my every need.

I have certainly experienced my share of administrators in the academia who changed things to adjust curriculum to the latest teaching methods coming from the most liberal college professors in the nation who needed something to do in order to justify their huge salaries, their tenure, and publications. "Publish or perish" liberal ideas was paramount, teaching was an inconvenience.

Others made changes because they could and were on a power trip. Absolute power is quite intoxicating to liberals. After the buzz wore off, when the student results were worse, we would always revert to the old tried and true teaching methods. In the meantime, students suffered.

The accusation from the most entitled generation of Americans, the Millenials, that we are too old to understand the need for protecting the environment, is bizarre. We did more to safeguard nature in one month than they did their entire spoiled lives.

I never had a washer and dryer until my mid-twenties. Most of the generation I grew up with still do not have a washing machine much less a dryer. We used the clothesline, the very one the Home Owners Associations consider unsightly and forbid it.

A vacuum cleaner was a pipe dream. We beat the dust out of the old carpets with a wooden paddle, while hanging wool rugs on a metal bar or on the balcony. Refrigerators were out of reach for most people. We bought food every day or used the windowsill in wintertime. We never heard of freezers, hair driers, curlers, and other electrical household appliances Americans have and do not appreciate.

We did not have a TV until I was in high school, much less a TV in every room. The one person on the block who had TV first, held parties for everybody to watch a movie or soccer on weekends.

We did not feel entitled and did not demand reparations from the nationalities that invaded our lands, enslaved us, and confiscated our properties. We started over, worked hard, and saved what we could. It was shameful to steal from others.

We walked everywhere, took the bus, and the train, if we could afford it. No school bus picked us up and dropped us at the door every day. We walked. Nobody fed us free lunches at school or any lunches for that matter. The government was subsidizing the prices of our food so why would they also feed us free.

If we give food stamps to 43 million people, why do we have to feed the very same families' kids three free meals at school? What happened to parental responsibility? Since when does the government become the sole provider for one's livelihood? Is Uncle Sam now our sole provider? Have we become so helpless?

The ignorant Occupiers who protest Wall Street and the rich, busy themselves with the latest electronic gadgets made possible by the opportunity found under capitalism to develop and market ideas that are forbidden in totalitarian societies. Instead of pointing fingers at the rich and demanding their wealth, ask the President where the promised shovel-ready jobs are.

Difficult times are appropriate moments to accept welfare until one's economic situation improves. However, to become a life-long welfare recipient of government dole while contributing nothing to society is not acceptable in a free society. Sadly, we are becoming entirely dependent on government. We have become a dumbed-down entitlement society. The ruling class encourages mediocrity, dependence, poverty, criminality, and laziness.

Our society provides ample opportunities for every citizen to become the best they can be, but it does not guarantee equal outcome. You must work hard to achieve your goals and you are not entitled to someone else's labor just because you have made bad choices or you had bad luck. Life is not fair and we do not need government and liberals to make everything and everyone economically equal by punishing the achievers.

Conservatives think logically and are not ruled by emotion. Liberals, on the other hand, propose lunatic ideas such as establishing a BBC/PBS International University to spread Marxism, or banning the tourist and travel industries entirely because it is human collective madness to use energy in such a wasteful way. In the liberal illogical mind, forbidding mobility and controlling people with Marxist drivel and indoctrination are necessary in order to establish their envisioned global primitive and just society. The liberals' hero, Karl Marx, was a bum.

I am a conservative because I take pride in a good day's work and enjoy the financial and non-monetary rewards that come with hard work. My heart swells with pride that I can take care of my family. I am satisfied that I enlightened someone's life. Perhaps I helped them understand a difficult aspect of economics; maybe I showed them how to edit a paper, taught them a few words in a foreign language, or instructed them on how to properly study for a test.

I will reluctantly accept help if I am too sick and unable to provide for my loved ones and myself. Nobody owes me anything and I do not feel entitled to someone else's wealth, nor am I envious of someone's good fortune, education, entrepreneurship, risk-taking, or hard work.

I will never be a liberal because I have too much pride, I want to be free, and I believe strongly that only God can take life away.

Being Poor in America

Liberal social critic Michael Harrington published in 1962 a book entitled, "The Other America," describing those who were ill clothed and fed in the land of plenty, in a nation where obesity was a problem. Harrington proclaimed that there was a **"cycle of poverty"** that could be broken only by *government action.* His book profoundly influenced Lyndon Johnson who declared **"War on Poverty"** in 1964. Forty-seven years later, after we have spent trillions of dollars on the poor, so-called downtrodden Americans, we have lost the war on poverty.

The government adopted an official definition of poverty. In 1964, those families who made less than $3,000 a year were poor. President Johnson's goal was to get every American above the **poverty line** by 1976, the bicentennial of our country. The poverty line was adjusted every year to reflect changes in the cost of living.

The federal poverty line for a family of four in 2011 was set at $22,350. Each state had a lower or higher number, depending on their cost of living adjustment.

According to the federal government, 35 percent of the poor are children. This is an interesting data to ponder since children do not live alone, do not earn an income, and few are likely to have accumulated wealth. If they do, they cannot touch it until they become of age.

The 2010 Census Bureau's exaggerated definition of poverty includes 40 million Americans in the category of poor. These families have air conditioning, TV, cable television, refrigerators, vacuum cleaners, XBOX game players, washers and dryers, a heated home, adequate shelter, and microwaves.

Progressives bemoan the homelessness, illegitimacy, drug dependency, and ill health of the poor. Conservatives argue that official data badly overstate the numbers because official definition should include free goods received such as education, public housing, healthcare, food, cell phones, and other assistance.

If you ask ten individuals if they are poor, you are likely to get the same answer, yes, they are poor but for 10 different reasons. Some will actually say they are cash poor in the bank, some are cash poor in their pockets, some consider themselves poor because they do not own a home or the car of their dreams, some because they do not have enough scholarships or grants to go to college, others who do not have wealth, cannot go on vacations ever or as often as they want, or cannot retire to the golf range.

People confuse cash with income and accumulated wealth. Cash is something on hand to spend, income is derived through hard work on a bi-weekly, monthly, or yearly basis, and accumulated wealth is either inherited or derived from hard work and entrepreneurship over time, taking risk with business ideas and investing capital to bring ideas to reality.

The optimistic economic concept of poverty is absolute – if you fall short of a minimum standard of living, you are poor. If you pass this standard by one dollar, you are no longer poor. The pessimistic concept of poverty is relative – if you fall too far behind the average income, you are poor. Absolute poverty is obviously arbitrary. Who is to decide what is too far behind? I am sure Romanians would be very happy and would consider themselves prosperous to have much less than the poor in this country. Americans in the 1900s would have considered themselves rich to have what the poor in America have today.

Poverty is determined culturally and is thus a relative concept. European Union (EU) determines the poverty line to be half the average national income. If EU becomes richer, the poverty line rises and thus people become richer.

The lines become blurred and thus poverty becomes **income inequality,** making progressives scream that we must bring about **social justice**, taking from the rich and give to the poor, the tenets of Marxism.

Our market system **does not guarantee** income equality. Progressives write and talk at nauseam about the distribution of income in the U.S. having grown substantially more unequal since the 1980s. Liberals demand that incomes be equal. If their demands were rational, they would understand that it is impossible, even under their beloved communism to have income equality. There are many reasons why incomes are unequal:

- People have different capabilities, some can do math quicker, speak better, run faster, ski better, type more accurately, paint better, have better entrepreneurial skills, better IQs, are more inventive, more creative, more musical than others

- People can work longer hours than others, labor more intensely – such disparities of income are largely voluntary
- People take risks with stock market, a new business – Bill Gates and Steve Jobs come to mind
- People work in dangerous jobs that are reflected in compensating wage differentials – people who work the night shift receive higher wages
- People who are schooled or better trained receive higher pay; they have sacrificed current income to study in order that they may receive a higher income in the future
- More work experience commands higher wages
- People who have inherited wealth do not necessarily derive their income from work – think of the Rockefellers
- People who inherit human capital wealth command higher wages – persons whose families have attended Ivy League colleges will likely benefit from this tradition and attend the same college, thus the process will result in higher wages for them.
- Luck is an insidious cause of wage differentials – good or bad fortune can help one digger to find gold or oil and another to find water or just rocks

People in general understand why incomes are unequal and find these variables rational. Liberals tend to find these differentials intolerable and **"socially unjust,"** claiming discrimination with every perceived wrong. Economic discrimination does exist and may or may not be deliberate.

Economic discrimination is said to exist when "equivalent factors of production receive different payments for equal contributions to output." In real life, it is difficult to decide when two factors of production are "equivalent." It is not called discriminatory if a woman with a high school diploma receives less compensation than a man with a college degree. If a man and a woman have the same education but the man may have 10 years more experience than the woman does, and they receive different wages for this reason, is it discriminatory?

If men and women were equally productive but received different wages, then that would be discriminatory. It is quite impossible to measure productivity in many white-collar jobs.

To combat poverty, besides the obvious better education, the government implemented programs collectively called welfare such as

Aid to Families with Dependent Children (AFDC), replaced by Clinton's Temporary Assistance to Needy Families (TANF), food stamps (currently 43 million people are on food stamps, the highest on record), WIC, and Medicaid. The problem with these programs is that it encourages people to remain on the dole. As their incomes rise, they are taxed some and the incentive to work becomes quite weak. Furthermore, the more out-of-wedlock children they have in the absence of a father, the more benefits they receive. Government becomes the daddy, thus destroying the nucleus of the family.

The Earned Income Tax Credit was also established to combat poverty. As earnings rise from zero to some threshold, the federal government supplements the earnings of the poor by giving them a grant proportional to their earnings. The EITC dates back to 1975 and it is now "America's biggest income-support program, reaching over 22 million families."

The federal government, in its quest to control every aspect of our lives, made it illegal to discriminate. The Civil Rights Act of 1964 outlawed many forms of discrimination and established the Equal Employment Opportunity Commission (EEOC).

Affirmative Action was controversial from the start and it remains so today. Many claim that it is insufficient "social justice," while others claim that it is "numerical quotas and compulsory hiring of unqualified workers simply because they are female or minority."

Proponents argue, "affirmative action is needed to redress past wrongs and to prevent discriminatory employers from claiming that they are unable to find qualified minority or female employees."

Robert Rector of the Heritage Foundation states, "Census officials continue to grossly exaggerate the numbers of the poor, creating a false picture in the public mind of widespread material deprivation."

"Most news stories on poverty feature homeless families, people living in crumbling shacks, or lines of the downtrodden eating in soup kitchens," Rector says. "The actual living conditions of America's poor are far different from these images."

In spite of our escalating debt ceiling problems, we spend nearly one trillion dollars a year on welfare although many recipients are not the typical poor in need of government assistance. Many people on welfare and Medicaid drive up to pharmacy windows to pick up their prescriptions in brand-new expensive SUVs. In the recession of 2009, only about 4 percent of the poor became temporarily homeless.

Rector and co-author Rachel Sheffield wrote, "The media 'amplified' the Census Bureau's annual misrepresentation of poverty over the past 40 years. News reports routinely suggest that poor Americans typically are homeless and hungry — and U.S. foes and rivals such as Iran, China, and Russia are delighted to report the same."

"Regrettably, most discussions of poverty in the U.S. rely on sensationalism, exaggeration, and misinformation," Rector says. "But an effective anti-poverty policy must be based on an accurate assessment of actual living conditions and the causes of deprivation."

Are we then truly poor in the U.S. and why is the federal government deliberately keeping a large portion of U.S. population dependent on welfare and other social programs while bankrupting the country with its out-of-control spending?

IMMIGRATION

Explosion of Immigrants

Census Bureau disclosed that the number of foreign-born residents in the United States, legal and illegal, reached 40 million in 2010, the highest in American history. Fourteen million immigrants came to America between 2000-2010. The Bureau reports that, of the 40 million total foreign-born residents, 10-12 million are likely illegal.

According to the Census Bureau, America's immigrant population has doubled since 1990 and tripled since 1980. Some states experienced more than 75 percent increase in immigrant population:
- Alabama (92 percent)
- South Carolina (88 percent)
- Tennessee (82 percent)
- Arkansas (79 percent)
- Kentucky (75 percent)

The immigrant population in the country grew 28 percent from 2000-2010. The current share of immigrants when compared to the total U.S. population is 12.9 percent. We have had a larger share of immigrant population in the early 1900s but the U.S. population was much smaller then.

California (27 percent), Texas, Florida (19 percent), New York (22 percent), Nevada (18.8 percent), and New Jersey (21 percent) have the highest percentages of foreign-born residents.

According to a Newsmax report, Countries in Latin America represented 58 percent of the growth in immigrant population from 2000-2010. Mexico supplied nearly 12 million immigrants, followed by China, Hong Kong, Taiwan, India, Philippines, Vietnam, and El Salvador.

The federal government is bending over backwards to accommodate the estimated 12 million illegal aliens through back door amnesty. Since Congress has not acted to write amnesty legislation, a stealth amnesty began during the week of November 17, 2011 with the Department of Homeland Security (DHS) reviewing all deportations.

A nationwide "training program" will assure that agents and prosecuting attorneys will not remove "illegal immigrants who have not been convicted of crimes," although crossing the border illegally is a crime.

According to Judicial Watch, in 2010 a Texas newspaper published a story that DHS has systematically cancelled pending deportations. Judicial Watch pursued DHS records and sued them when the agency ignored a federal public records request.

The Commonwealth of Virginia's population grew by 2 million people in the 2000-2010 census, 25 percent of growth due to an influx of Hispanics. The Hispanic population grew from 3 percent in 2000 (160,000 people) to 300 percent (632,000 people) in 2010.

In 1990, the Hispanic population in Prince William County, Virginia, was 4 percent or 9,662. Today it is 81,460 and "accounting for almost 40 percent of total population growth in the county."

"Virginia House Bill 3202, signed into law by Democrat Governor Tim Kaine in 2007 with bi-partisan support, required 67 counties and cities to create Urban Development Areas (UDA) based on decennial population growth criteria."

"The Urban Development Areas must be able to accommodate high population growth and include features like 'pedestrian friendly' design, mixed use housing, and minimum housing densities that presume an urban landscape and encourage low-income subsidized housing." Interestingly, these are the same guidelines for Smart Growth of the United Nations Agenda 21.

"By demanding Urban Development Areas in counties with high population growth rates, the Virginia legislature is pandering to illegal immigrants." The character and the voting preference of Virginia's rural counties have changed. When the stealth amnesty is complete, all newly-minted American citizens will vote Democrat. However, with all the leftist vote fraud across the country and Democrat-driven redistricting, amnesty may not even be necessary to "fundamentally" alter the American voting landscape.

What do we do with all the illegal immigrants in the country? As New Gingrich said in a presidential debate, we cannot throw out people and their families who have been in this country illegally for 25 years. What if the "undocumented workers" had been in this country illegally for 15 years? What if they do not have a family? Who gets to decide and how? What is the cut-off point? Would amnesty not encourage more illegal aliens coming to the U.S.? That is exactly what happened when

Ronald Reagan gave amnesty to 2 million illegal aliens during his administration. Reagan regretted his decision and admitted later that it was a failure.

What is the rate of assimilation for foreign-born residents into our society? Are illegal aliens interested in assimilating and learning our language and culture? Do they respect America, its Constitution, its flag, national anthem, the pledge of allegiance, and our way of life?

Judging by the fact that illegal aliens are translating our national anthem into Spanish, our government prints everything in Spanish at huge cost to taxpayers, corporate America advertises in English and Spanish as if we already are a bi-lingual country, and American students are forced to pledge allegiance to Mexico during Spanish classes in Texas, I would say that the answer is no. The pandering left and the Marxist academia promote multi-culturalism in spite of the fact that it is an admitted huge failure in Europe.

The "Oregonian" reported the success of Oregon students in English Language Learner programs (ELL). Last year, of the 65,000 students enrolled in ELL, only 10,379 were deemed proficient in English. That is an 84 percent failure rate. School districts receive $3,000 per ELL student from the state and another $150 from the federal government. Such funding takes away school resources from English-speaking American students.

ELL programs, heavily promoted by the Department of Education bureaucrats and teachers, encourage a bilingual, divided society, rather than a society united by a common language and culture.

"ELL programs are overwhelmingly provided for Spanish-speakers, encouraging a divisive, disruptive, ethnocentric activity." Foreign-born students feel entitled to receive such benefits and college aid provided by the forced generosity of the American taxpayers. However, no such largesse is extended to American citizens. They must work hard in order to pay for the entitled illegal aliens.

Michael Savage offered a simple solution to our quandary: "borders, language, and culture." Enforce and protect the borders, require English only language proficiency, and promote, teach, and respect our monolithic culture.

Citizen U.S.A.

My American citizenship was an arduous journey, years in the making. It took mountains of paperwork on both sides of the Atlantic. Papers had to be translated from and into English, notarized, fiscally stamped, taxed, and approved. Appointments had to be made with various officials and officers of the law.

Security Police interrogations and screenings were performed. Were you ever a Communist, how much debt did you have, did you have a savings account, did you have a job, who was going to support you, who was going to pay medical bills, did I speak English, did I pass the American Government test, was I literate, and who was the president. And the questions never stopped until the American government was sure that I would not be a burden on the American taxpayers and would be a contributing citizen to this wonderful constitutional republic.

Things have changed dramatically. Now prospective and future American citizens come to hearings with translators in tow. The American government must provide translations for every piece of paper Spanish speakers have to fill out. Seeking American citizenship, some immigrants know very little nor care about their newly adopted country. Their main goal is to bring the third world dictatorship-nation they just fled from to America and force their culture onto the host.

If foreign nationals come to court, although some of them have lived in the U.S. for 23 years and speak English, they prefer to give testimony in Spanish, out of respect for their first language. What about the respect for those present in the courtroom who conduct business in the language of the land, English?

Voting rolls are translated into Spanish and school curriculum is provided in two languages, at great expense to the taxpayer. Hospitals must provide translators to illegal aliens who flock to the emergency rooms as if they are doctors' offices. Companies display every sign in their stores both in English and Spanish and phone calls are answered by pressing one for English.

The ceremony of becoming a citizen is a sacred one – one swears allegiance to America, to the republic and everything it stands for. You swear to honor and preserve its culture, its symbols, its flag, and its national anthem. You do not have the right to wave and display the flag of your former country in the face of Americans while telling them that America will soon be yours because it was stolen from you.

Few borders in the world have been adjudicated by entirely peaceful means. Many countries' boundaries were carved out after a conflict, armistice, as a purchase, or other forms of forced distribution.

The Washington Post wrote in a recent column about "Citizen U.S.A.," a 53-minute film made by Nancy Pelosi's daughter, Alexandra. The columnist stated that we have "not learned much" from this film other than "how easy it is to take your citizenship for granted."

The writer was apparently fascinated not by the momentous occasion of becoming a citizen of the greatest nation on earth, but by the "wide and occasionally bizarre variety of amateur entertainment that precedes a swearing-in ceremony: choirs of elderly patriots, story tellers, a woman doing a song and an audience participation dance, involving red, white, and blue paper plates…"

The Washington Post article continued that, although we are a "nation at war" and "griped out," the swear-in ceremony "will give you hope in this 235-year experiment we've got going here."

I was under the impression that we lived in the most successful nation on earth, not an experiment.

The critic was annoyed with the film because only "passing references were made to current immigration debates, particularly when Alexandra Pelosi visits Arizona and there's a mob outside the building, counter-protesting the state's recently harsh-ified immigration laws."

The writer apparently ignored the fact that the debate in Arizona is over, it is the law, the majority has decided. It is hard for progressives to admit defeat when their minority ranks do not get their wishes. Only in a liberal mind is a law that already exists at the federal level in more stringent form, harsh. Only in a liberal mind, breaking the law to come to this country by crossing the border illegally, should be rewarded with instant citizenship.

The writer claimed that the film, "Citizen U.S.A., is without an agenda, open to all." His frame of reference is most telling. "Apart from the occasional debate over whether the United States needs to replace the national anthem with something more singable than "The Star Spangled Banner," one song was apparently long ago chosen for that task by the people in charge of swearing-in ceremonies, Lee

Greenwood's sap-tastic 1984 ballad "God Bless the U.S.A."

I was not aware that the national anthem was open for debate. As a proud American citizen by choice, I cherish and honor it. Perhaps it is debatable in the progressive mind and the minds of the newly minted Americans interviewed for the movie. Proposing to change our national anthem and still trying to debate the immigration law that has already passed in Arizona, does not seem to me that the movie has no agenda.

The newly minted citizens should give us hope that our 235-year old Constitutional Republic will thrive in spite of its financial troubles created by schizophrenic economic policies of past and present administrations.

The torch of freedom of the land of plenty, of the shining city on the hill that everyone wants to immigrate to, will be passed on by this proud American to my children, my former students, and all proud Americans who make this country exceptional.

Multiculturalism and English First

To become part of the fabric of this society and its melting pot, you have to learn English. It is illogical to refuse adopting the language of the majority – there are too many missed opportunities and self-marginalization in a society where the sky is the limit.

If your goal is to reject 235 years of U.S. history and culture by changing it into your vision of Latin hood, then Spanish-only barrios make sense. There is also the option of going back where you came from if this country's customs, language, religion, and culture offend you.

English is not our official language. Any other country in the world has an official language. The modern obstacle for passage of English as an official language is Executive Order 13166, signed by former President Bill Clinton.

The United States is "officially multilingual by requiring the government, all businesses that work with the government, and anybody receiving any form of federal benefit, to provide all of their services in the language of choice of any recipient."

During President Bush's administration, Executive Order 13166 grew, aided by the U.S. Office of Civil Rights. Nobody knows why Bush did not repeal it. We can speculate that he was pandering to the Latino vote.

"Executive Order 13166 was enforced when challenged by radical pro-Hispanic organizations seeking to weaken America's one-language policies." This Presidential Order is still the law of the land and, if fully implemented, could cause a catastrophe of massive proportions.

Experts agree that all levels of government, federal, state, local, schools, hospitals, churches, nonprofit organizations, and even doctors could be forced to provide any language expertise under this order. The economic cost would be staggering.

We already spend billions translating into Spanish everything from store advertising, voting rolls, textbooks, instructions, government forms, immigration tests and papers, textbooks, DMV documents, driving tests, nationalization papers, citizenship tests, swearing-in ceremonies, hospital procedures, phone robotic messages, press 1 for Spanish. We cheat our own children out of a decent education in order to provide for the children of illegal aliens. People die because of improperly translated medical information. We have to unite behind our one common language, English.

Rep. Peter King (R-NY) introduced **H.R.1307, English First.** If passed, this bill would nullify Executive Order 13166 and English will become the official language. Congressman King's bill states explicitly "that Executive Order 13166 shall have no force or effect." Whether it will pass or not, it depends on the strong anti-American, Latino pro-communist lobby that prefers Spanish as the language of the Reconquista land.

Maryland is usually the first state in the nation that passes anti-American, pro-Agenda 21, pro-illegal immigration laws in the nation. It is no surprise that it has recently passed the Dream Act, in-state tuition for illegal immigrant, college bound children.

It may seem an insignificant law since only a few hundred illegal aliens will benefit in the beginning. Gustavo Torres, with his Casa de Maryland, wants to take his immigration Dream Act fight nationally. Deporting 400,000 aliens annually is an insufferable number of potential union dues-paying workers and Democrat voters.

Torres is Executive Director for Casa de Maryland, situated in Langley Park, a mansion he purchased from Gregg Clickstein for $1. Casa now has a budget of $6 million, half of which comes from local, state, and federal tax appropriations, helping illegal immigration.

Big Labor bosses, especially SEIU, like-minded politicians, clergy, and cunning progressives promote illegal immigrants rights at the expense of American law and American taxpayers. Eliseo Medina, secretary-treasurer of SEIU said, "The people who started this plantation, if only they had known it, would become the People's home." Suddenly, illegal immigrants are now "we the People" in Casa de Maryland.

Republican state Delegate Pat McDonough objects to the local, state, and federal money funding the house itself, to the legal and other services provided to 20,000 illegal immigrants annually. "Gustavo has created a sanctuary state." "The Governor does his bidding. The politicians who control power in the State of Maryland do his bidding…And his success has caused financial and personal heartbreak for the State of Maryland." "They are a globally significant organization."

Casa de Maryland is in part the success of the heavy lobbying of Gustavo Torres, a Medellin, Colombia, legal immigrant. The Washington Post and the liberal media compare Torres to Che Guevara, the iconic figure of the communist/progressive movement in this country who disregards the fact that Che was the butcher of thousands and thousands of innocents who opposed his Marxist doctrine.

Torres and Casa de Maryland rallied "undocumented workers" as the progressives like to call them, to protest apartment living conditions. Illegal aliens felt entitled to housing on par with Americans and demanded same rights as American citizens.

Gregg Clickstein, who sold the mansion for $1 to Torres said, "This nation of immigrants... and this new wave of immigrants, and having the opportunity to assimilate and be great Americans. And it really just touched me." That sounds idealistic and noble, however most illegal aliens have no intention of assimilating, they want to bring their native countries culture of poverty, corruption and oppression with them under the banner of the Democrat party.

Gustavo Torres talks about "la lista negra" from his native Colombia. "If I did these kinds of things in Colombia, I'd have been killed a long time ago." He is now cunningly using our tolerant laws and freedoms against legal Americans, trying to transform our country into the Colombia he fled.

The effort to pass Maryland Dream Act, the in-state tuition bill for illegal immigrant children paid off, it passed 27-19 in Senate and 74-65 in House.

Montgomery County, Maryland, has a Latino Health Initiative, lobbying for free health care for illegal immigrants. They already have access to free health care in our nation's emergency rooms. If Americans have an emergency, they must wait eight hours or longer until all illegal immigrants' sniffles and colds are seen by an emergency room doctor. Should you have a real emergency, you must wait your turn.

Member dues, corporations, and foundations such as Morris and Gwendolyn Cafritz, Harry and Jeanette Weinberg, Ford, the Open Society Institute of Baltimore, Bank of America, Wells Fargo, and CITGO also support Casa de Maryland. Who knew that Hugo Chavez had his communist tentacles in Maryland?

Torres, who makes $86,000 a year as Executive Director, talks about "positive social change," euphemism for communism, and his aims for Casa's influence – White House, Homeland Security, and Congress. It is abundantly clear that his aim is not to adjust and adapt to our capitalist system but change his adopted country into the communist "paradise" many illegal aliens have fled. Casa's mission statement is "to create a more just society," code words for communism.

Casa de Maryland attracted a "team of true-believing organizers, fundraisers, lawyers and specialists who are the envy of liberal nonprofits in the region." Cecilia Munoz, White House director of intergovernmental affairs, and Thomas Perez, assistant attorney general for civil rights are alumni of Casa's board.

Torres' goal is to "build a powerful movement of immigrants and other minorities including the African American community to fight for justice – and they decide what justice means." This sounds to me like a call to communist revolution.

According to their union, Casa de Maryland's workers enjoy fully funded health insurance. Part-time teachers give lessons in English to those who desire to learn the language.

Before the Dream Act passed, Torres consulted the students if they agreed with the "tough" requirement that students or their parents must have filed a Maryland tax return. Torres wanted to know if they accepted the compromise. Asking an illegal teenager for permission to pursue a political course? Asking an illegal alien who broke the law to accept a compromise?

Delegate McDonough was disappointed when the bill passed. His speech was the voice shouting in the desert, "Maryland is becoming Disneyland for illegal aliens… Now there are 300,000 illlegals in Maryland. When do you reach sticker shock?.. They are not fighting for civil rights, they are fighting for civil wrongs…"

Should we not have an official language? Should we fully adopt the illegal alien and liberal multiculturalism agenda that is currently destroying Europe? Should we not fight to preserve America as our fore fathers founded it? Should we not preserve the rule of law and our Constitution? Should we give in to illegal immigrants because they feel that we have stolen their land and it is their right to get it back through any means necessary? Are we that busy and lazy that we are not noticing what is happening to our country?

Broken Immigration, Broken Education

Our broken education system and the immigration without integration issues were brought to the forefront once more in the recent fight of a woman in Arizona who wished to run for a city council seat.

According to the Phoenix Sun, Cabrera did not speak proficient English and used an interpreter to communicate, in spite of the fact that she is a graduate of Kofa High School in Yuma.

She acknowledged that her English skills were limited but, in an area where Spanish is the predominant language, it is not necessary to speak English in order to serve the population's interests. This statement begs the question, who is going to represent the interests of the American citizens who are here lawfully and do speak English? In addition, why did she receive a high school diploma from an accredited high school if she does not speak English?

Social promotion in our schools on any level is wrong, yet liberal academics have been pushing this issue for many years, diluting the quality of graduates to the point that some are unable to read, write, or do simple arithmetic.

"State law requires elected officials to know English, but Cabrera's attorneys claim the law does not define proficiency in the language." (Phoenix Sun)

A socio-linguist expert, who administered three tests to Cabrera, an English-speaking skills test, a reading skills test, and an English comprehension test, deemed her unable to answer questions in English.

"Cabrera's lawyers said the action against their client was politically motivated." Whatever the claim, the fact remains that, as a member of the council, she would be unable to serve her English speaking constituents without the help of an interpreter. Taxpayer dollars would have to provide her with an interpreter on a daily basis and such services are expensive.

Liberals love to defend and hinder assimilation into this country in spite of ample evidence from the failed and disastrous European model of allowing immigrants to bring their countries, their customs, and their language with them into self-isolating ghettoes.

President Merkel of Germany and President Sarkozy of France have admitted in separate statements that multiculturalism is a failure in Europe, socially, economically, and politically, and it is not sustainable. "The hostility of young minority men toward authority across communities in Europe" has escalated, the deep-seated antipathy leading to frequent and deadly violence.

Socioeconomic as well as linguistic integration are necessary for a group to progress and thrive within the same borders. Expecting the local population to provide expensive translators to a subculture that refuses to learn the language of the land is detrimental to both groups, preventing inclusion and economic success.

The Roman Empire had established Latin as the administrative language of the conquered lands. They viewed communication as an important ingredient of economic success and governance. Many tribes reluctantly accepted Latin but transformed it to suit their native languages and dialects. The result was the six Latin-based romance languages that are spoken today: French, Italian, Spanish, Romanian, Portuguese, and Romansh. Romansh is spoken in a particular canton in Switzerland. Interestingly, although the Roman Empire disappeared in the West in 476 A.D., scholars across Europe had used Latin for centuries afterwards to promote writing and learning, while the Catholic Church published documents in Latin and used it ceremonially.

Alfred the Great (849-899), the only Anglo-Saxon scholar king that we know could read and write, was convinced that learning was the key to a better life for all. He commissioned the translation of instructive books from Latin to Old English. It is interesting to note, although modern English is a Germanic language, 51 percent of its vocabulary comes from Latin. The Roman Empire disappeared long time ago but its language lives on.

I do not know the status of every person who does not speak English in this country, whether they are here legally or illegally. A significant portion of the 10.8 million illegal immigrants inside the United States entered with a valid visa and stayed after their visas expired. A large percentage hides within enclaves and never learns English, depriving themselves of better social and economic opportunities.

Furthermore, the current administration, by suing various states who passed legislation to enforce immigration laws, is giving the signal that entering the U.S. illegally and staying indefinitely will not be penalized but rewarded through stealth amnesty. When our economy will improve, we will see more illegal immigration since economic need is the primary reason for illegal immigration from Latin America.

A guest worker program would help establish respect for the rule of law and fill the employers' needs for seasonal workers. The Bracero Program (*bracero* means *strong-arm* in Spanish), a series of laws and diplomatic agreements with Mexico instituted by FDR in1942, worked well until 1964 when it was canceled.

Visa programs for temporary or seasonal agricultural workers must be streamlined. E-Verify system and Self Check to correct errors and issues should be encouraged.

Amnesty granted to 2-3 million illegal immigrants in 1986 made the situation much worse, encouraging a new wave of illegal immigration. President Reagan admitted the failure.

If the economic situation of a country is good, there is no need to migrate illegally to the U.S. We do not see many Chileans here because their economy is thriving when compared to other Latin American countries. Promoting economic development and good governance in Latin America would go a long way to stem illegal immigration.

According to the Heritage Foundation, the "push-pull effect caused by the combination of slow economic growth in Latin America and the need for workers in the United States" is a large contributor to illegal immigration.

No matter how we view or present the legal and illegal immigration issues, the facts and statistics show the burden on the U.S. economy:

- 400,000 illegal immigrant women give birth to "anchor-babies" who become automatic U.S. citizens
- One in every four inmates in federal prisons is an illegal immigrant (U.S. Government Accountability Office)
- 50-60 percent illegal immigrants are high school dropouts (Heritage Foundation)
- Illegal immigrants come from Mexico (58 percent), Latin America (23 percent), Asia, Europe, and Africa (18 percent)

A controversial proposal to grant illegal immigrant students in-state tuition passed in twelve states as of July 2011. As this law attempts to improve and address the education of illegal immigrants, opposing groups highlight the fact that their parents have broken the law in crossing the border illegally and are thus not entitled to same rights as American citizens. The controversy is not likely to diminish, particularly when generations of "anchor-babies" turn eighteen and demand family integration and full rights as American citizens.

Alabama Immigration Law

Living in the South most of my adult life, I have experienced an explosion of illegal immigrant population in the nineties. Border laws were enforced in the 70s and 80s. It was hard to become a legal resident, much less an American citizen. People used legal channels and waited patiently for the resolution of their visas.

We did not have to speak a foreign language in our own country or press 2 for Spanish. There were no duplicate signs in Spanish in every large store. Forms were not printed in Spanish and doctors were not obligated to hire translators. Illegal immigrants could not vote and were not encouraged to do so. Nobody dared to demonstrate in front of Americans while waving their countries' flags, shouting that America is theirs and the old gringos should roll over and die, it is time for young Mexicans to rule. La Raza was not stoking hatred in the open and it did not have a voice in the White House.

We were not spending $25 per hour on translators to tutor illegal immigrants' children in Spanish after school to read and do simple math. ESL was not touted everywhere. Legal immigrants made an effort to learn English and adapted to the laws and culture of America. They assimilated and became part of the American dream. We had fewer barrios and Latino gangs. The federal government enforced the borders.

The stakes are high today to put a stop to illegal immigration that is threatening the functioning of our orderly society. It is up to individual states to do so since the federal government has relinquished its duty to defend the borders. If we no longer have safe and secure borders and the Mexican government tries to dictate to us what constitutes America, do we still have sovereignty?

Arizona's immigration law was immediately challenged in court. Conservatives cheered while liberals screamed racism in tune with the Department of Justice. The law did not violate anybody's rights but reinforced the rules that the federal government should have enforced but failed to do. Arizona had become a war zone along its border with Mexico.

The 2010 Arizona law found that "there is a compelling interest in the cooperative enforcement of federal immigration laws throughout all of Arizona." The provisions of this act "are intended to work together to discourage and deter the unlawful entry and presence of aliens and economic activity by persons unlawfully present in the United States." Immediately, all the liberal media denounced it as racist, profiling, and bigoted, and the Department of Justice filed suit against the state.

Alabama passed its immigration law in June 2011 and it was immediately opposed by the Hispanic lobby, La Raza, LULAC (League of United Latin American Citizens), corrupt business interests, and the open-borders Justice Department.

Alabama's immigration law was similar to Arizona's law because it allowed local law enforcement to ask for immigration papers during routine traffic stops.

Alabama further voided any contracts signed by illegal aliens, forbidding them from "mainstreaming" into communities. The law banned contracts between illegal aliens and any organization of the state government.

All incoming students had to prove immigration status before elementary and secondary schools could admit them. The state wanted to know eventually how much money was spent to educate illegal aliens.

The day the law went into effect, many classrooms were emptied as illegal aliens kept their children at home, citing a hostile learning environment. Yet American children must show proof of residence at the beginning of each school year in order to enroll in a particular district.

I am not sure if Alabama will be able to overturn the 1981 policy upheld by the Supreme Court that required all 50 states to provide free public education to illegal aliens. The Court ruled that "no substantial state interest" was proven when Texas tried to deny free public education to illegal aliens. Perhaps providing a figure of billions of dollars a year might persuade the court.

As liberals promoted the failed European multiculturalism model, 87 percent of Americans believed that English should be the official language of the United States (Rasmussen Reports).

We are a nation of immigrants but we have followed the law and assimilated into this country, "one united people, speaking the same language, professing the same religion, attached to the same principles of government, very similar in their manners and customs." (Federalist Papers, John Jay)

When the influx was disproportionately from one area, laws were written to curtail it. The 1965 Immigration Act (Hart-Cellar Act) caused a surge of Latin American and Asian immigrants for decades. The Hart-Cellar Act allowed more immigrants from third world countries and a separate quota for refugees. Residence was granted based on skill and family reunification.

The "Fast and Furious" scandal served as evidence to the corruption and lack of protection of our borders when drug cartels made frequent incursions into U.S. territory. The results were deadly - U.S. law enforcement officers and innocent citizens falling victims during drug runs and battles over territory.

It was alleged that ATF illegally facilitated the transfer of thousands of guns to drug cartels in Mexico, with the knowledge of the Justice Department, in order to trace gang members through the U.S. registered guns.

The evidence pointed to the Obama administration providing guns to Mexican drug lords with the intent of blaming American gun ownership and the Second Amendment rights for violent crimes committed in Mexico.

The issues of immigration rest on a few simple facts that liberals ignore when they call illegal immigrants "undocumented workers:"

- It is illegal and a crime to cross the border of another country without proper visas and documentation.
- There is no automatic right to American citizenship.
- Illegal aliens do not have the right to vote but they do vote for the Democrat Party
- Aliens flee from third world countries and poverty, yet they want to bring it here
- Illegal aliens change our voting trends to fit the Democrats nanny state agenda.
- Illegal immigrants are not entitled to any generous social welfare programs, free medical care, housing, and equal protection under the law on par with U.S. citizens.
- Illegal immigrants are taking jobs that unemployed Americans were previously doing
- Illegal immigrants are driving wages down.
- Immigrants who are here illegally have committed a crime that is punishable quite severely in their own countries.
- U.S. taxpayers should not provide free education, medical care,

welfare, housing, and other social programs for illegal immigrants.

Our country is broke and hard-working Americans who pay taxes are tired of being the silent majority who pays the bills while liberals, the Democrat Party, and Washington are ignoring their voices. More states like Alabama and Arizona should adopt laws that check the status of immigrants in this country. We must restore law and order and take our borders back. Without borders, we are no longer a sovereign nation.

Democrats Import Illegal Voters With Communicable Diseases

America was built on the backs, hands, and minds of legal immigrants. We all came from somewhere else, except the Native Americans. We fled from religious persecution, communist tyranny, oppressive monarchies and regimes, legal entanglements, murder raps, theft, moral and financial responsibility to others.

We longed for the lure of riches and unbound freedom, but most of all, we desired the opportunity to be better off than our poor but hardworking families.

Lady Liberty welcomed us all, initially at Ellis Island, where thousands and thousands of newly arrived would-be Americans, gaunt and ragged from the arduous Atlantic passage remained on board three or four days in the harbor, then in quarantine before they were allowed inland. Wealthier crossers were processed on board the ship.

The would-be Americans, particularly the poor ones, suffered indignities at times but there was no ACLU to sue for their unjust treatment – they were thankful to be allowed onto the Land of Opportunity.

Proud, intelligent people with dreams, representing every country in the Old World, poured into America, bringing their cultures with them into the melting pot. They entered the enormous Ellis Island Receiving Station, the "Hall of Tears," as it was known, on "Heartbreak Island." Some family members were separated in the long lines, some were accepted, some rejected. Painful decisions had to be made quickly. People's names were entered in records misspelled or changed on purpose to suit the clerk's whims or inability to spell.

If they survived the treacherous Atlantic boat crossing and received a clean bill of health after the quarantine, they were free to explore their new country and make their dreams a reality through hard work, self-reliance, and perseverance. One such immigrant from Italy entered Ellis Island in 1902 and became a naturalized citizen in 1908.

In the last twenty years, immigration enforcement has become so lax that now, illegal immigrants are causing huge financial and social burdens on Americans in spite of La Rasa's claim that they do the jobs that Americans refuse to do. According to Democrats and the sycophant media, they are "undocumented workers," not illegal aliens. Only in the irrational progressive mind is someone, who is deliberately breaking the law of this country, an undocumented worker and must be rewarded with citizenship, free schooling, housing, food stamps, medical care, and free or in-state tuition for their children.

The liberal media refuses to discuss the burden millions of illegals place on this country's resources. They steal benefits from American citizens who have worked and paid Social Security and Medicaid taxes their entire lives and now are unable to draw benefits because the promised lock box is empty.

Hundreds and thousands of hospitals are strained or bankrupt because of the gratis care they must extend to illegal aliens. Having anchor babies in hospitals at taxpayer expense while the rest of Americans have to bankrupt themselves paying hospital bills is an injustice that lawmakers should have addressed long time ago.

An important issue that threatens the health of our nation is the communicable disease emergence, ills that have been eradicated in this country years ago.

Diseases such as tuberculosis, leprosy, pertussis or whooping cough, dengue fever, hepatitis, Chagas are prevalent in third world countries and are being transported to the U.S. via illegal immigrants who are not checked and given treatment or vaccinations.

Whooping cough is a disease associated with lack of sanitation in third world countries. Places of high concentration of illegals experience sudden problems of disease related to the developing world. The media in Smithtown, Long Island, reports "dozens" of whooping cough cases without making the connection to the culprits.

Dysentery, a deadly and very contagious disease for babies has been found to have infected a Phoenix Police officer. Not washing hands or laundering clothes aids in the spread of dysentery.

Malaria, which was eradicated sixty years ago, has re-appeared in California, New York City, and Houston, centers of high concentration of illegal aliens. Blood supplies infected with malaria have also been found in our cities.

Dengue fever, a virus-based disease spread by mosquitoes, which kills millions of children in third world countries, is now increasingly found in the U.S. where immigrants both legal and illegal congregate.

Leprosy currently known as Hansen's disease to hide its presence, is steadily rising with the invasion of illegal aliens and has accelerated since 2002.

"Hepatitis A-E is making people sick across the country. Chronically suffering illegal aliens who work in our restaurants, are sneaking across our borders from oil-rich Mexico to receive the free $1,500 per patient treatment. Not only do we pay for these treatments with our tax dollars but also we unwittingly become infected with hepatitis. Some forms are transmitted through unwashed hands while handling food, others through blood donations or contact with infected blood.

Tuberculosis, another deadly disease found in Mexico at a rate ten times higher than the U.S., is popping up nationwide wherever illegals are concentrated. More than half of the medical reporting districts in California have active TB cases. To make matters worse, a new incurable type of TB, XDR strain (extensively drug resistant) has appeared worldwide, including the United States.

Chagas disease, a tropical parasitic disease, previously found only in South America, Central America and Mexico, slowly destroys its victim's heart and other internal organs. The Chagas Disease Foundation said, "Chagas disease affects more people than any other infectious disease in Latin America and that it ranks as the largest cause of heart disease-induced deaths in the region. The result of a bug bite that leaves behind contaminated fecal matter, the disease can be spread through contaminated food, blood transfusion, organ donation, and mother to fetus.

According to CDC, "Since initiation of voluntary blood screening for Chagas disease in 2007, nearly 800 cases of confirmed Chagas disease have been detected at United States blood centers. The greatest numbers of positive donors, now deferred from donation, have been identified in those states with the largest populations of Latin American immigrants."

"Population migration can have a profound impact on movement of infectious diseases. The relative magnitude of movement of persons from Chagas endemic countries, including an estimated 18 million to the United States illustrates the problem." (CDC, 2009)

"Although historically Chagas disease has been considered restricted to Latin America, the disease is becoming a serious health issue in the United States because of the presence of a notable number of blood donors seropositive." (CDC, *Emerging Infectious Diseases,* Vol.16, No. 3, March 2010)

Legal immigrants have always been checked for communicable diseases before they were allowed to immigrate to the United States. We even require k-12 American students and college students to provide records and proof of immunization for certain childhood diseases. Why do we then think that it is a good idea to allow unchecked immigration and risk the health of our population for the sake of political votes and power?

The Democrat Party, Code Pink, ACLU, the environmental nuts with their debunked global warming, the Communist Party U.S.A. La Rasa, SEIU, other big unions, and like-minded progressives have openly embraced and invited illegal aliens into our country.

Democrats want the illegal aliens' fraudulent vote or legal vote at all costs, including our health, when they become automatic citizens through forced Amnesty and the Dream Act for illegal alien college students. Democrats, in their quest for totalitarian control, do not care that, in the process, they have invited into our country a host of health problems. This Pandora's Box of societal and financial ills caused by unchecked illegal immigration cannot be cured simply by spending money or signing more freedom-stealing Executive Orders.

Amnesty Above All

The plenary power of the U.S. Congress allows for passage of laws, levy of taxes, wage wars and hold in custody those who offend against its laws.

Under the Plenary Power Doctrine, Congress has the power to make immigration policy free from judicial review. This doctrine was established at the end of the nineteenth century. The Supreme Court declared that Congress had "plenary power" to regulate immigration, Indian tribes, and newly acquired territories.

The doctrine has basis in the concept that immigration is a question of national sovereignty, relating to a nation's right to define its own borders. "Courts generally refrain from interfering in immigration matters. To date there have been no successful challenges to federal legislation that refuses admission to classes of non-citizens or removes resident aliens."

"DHS, along with the Department of Justice, will be reviewing the current deportation caseload to clear out low-priority cases on a case-by-case basis and make more room to deport people who have been convicted of crimes or pose a security risk. In addition, they will take steps to keep low-priority cases out of the deportation pipeline in the first place. They will be applying common sense guidelines to these decisions, like a person's ties and contributions to the community, their family relationships and military service record." (Cecilia Munoz, August 18, 2011)

President Obama passed a document, a back door amnesty titled, *"Maximizing Public Safety and Better Focusing Resources,"* while suing Arizona and Alabama because they are enforcing immigration laws already on the books. As a DHS official said with a straight face, "This case-by-case approach will enhance public safety."

"Bowing to pressure from immigrant rights activists, the Obama administration said that it will halt deportation proceedings on a case-by-case basis against illegal immigrants who meet certain criteria, such as attending school, having family in the military or having primary responsibility for other family members 'care." (Washington Post, August 19, 2011)

The DHS and the White House have decided to take existing deportation cases and run them through a careful screening, which will cost money and time, and take resources from other areas. Suddenly, nobody is a threat to our national security; aliens can stay here for the duration. This is a usurpation of Congress' plenary power to decide who comes in and who does not.

Congress makes laws and the President executes those laws. The President is arrogating powers to himself to decide who comes into the country and who gets to stay. When we are trying to deliver quality education, health care, and other services to our citizens in a depressed economy, the notion that the president can let foreigners into our country at will and treat them equally with citizens, makes the president's discretion unlimited.

Our borders are out of control, our resources are strained, yet this administration is announcing that millions of aliens can stay, and states must provide for their free education, healthcare, employment, and housing.

The message to illegal immigrants is that if you get in, the chances of deportation are zero. We now have unlimited immigration, limited only by the number of people who are trying to come in.

The ability of our society to provide any kind of quality of life and services to future generations of Americans is uncertain. There are approximately 25 million unemployed looking for jobs, out of a labor force of approximately 155 million people. Nobody knows how many discouraged workers have dropped out of the labor market and are thus not counted. Jobs would be freed by deporting people who are here illegally.

We are a nation of immigrants and nobody can blame illegal immigrants who seek a better life, but there is a legal process to do so. Breaking the laws of our country is not the right way to do it. There are social and financial consequences to a blanket amnesty program:

- diminishes the legal citizenship process
- illegal aliens jump to the head of the line, at the expense of those who had to wait, spend money, and valuable time pursuing legal immigration
- takes away jobs from Americans at a time when we have high unemployment

- strains emergency medical services and bankrupts small hospitals (illegal immigrants use emergency rooms for regular doctor visits instead of a regular doctor whose fees would be much smaller but not free)
- depletes education funds, Social Security funds, housing funds, welfare funds, food stamps fund
- increases criminality (gangs and those who come here with nefarious intent)
- spreads unchecked diseases especially through unvaccinated children in school
- allows terrorists to enter freely into the United States

The regime is hiding behind the banner of "prosecutorial discretion." Each case must be judged on a case-by-case basis. Do we have the resources to do so when these people have broken the law by coming into the country illegally? There are different levels of criminality indeed, but once you break a law, you are a criminal. Crossing the border of any country illegally, whether for economic reasons or nefarious reasons, is a crime. Most countries, including Mexico, have serious punishments and immediate deportation for the offenders who cross their borders illegally.

What is the rationalization of blanket amnesty? Politicians and professional ethnic scam artists are screaming that they are not getting votes unless they are appeasing the Hispanic vote, partisan politics 101. There are no limits now to the Executive branch's authority to give out green cards to millions of new voters.

Never before has the Executive branch said indirectly to Congress and the American people that their wishes do not matter. Why would Congress bother to pass laws if the President is going to ignore them? Limitless, un-reviewed authority to run immigration policies outside of Congress' authority is soft tyranny. The rule of law cannot be ignored or self-determination as a nation no longer exists.

As the voice of the people no longer exists, legal challenges must be made so that status can be checked and deportation stream-lined in order to provide finality to the process. Existing immigration laws of the land must be enforced. Citizens must have legal standing, a standing clause that allows them to go to court to enjoin the president for stealing residency at the expense of the American people.

EDUCATION

American Ignorance

Americans are greatly misinformed when it comes to socialism and communism. Winston Churchill described the utopian ideology best, "socialism is a philosophy of failure, the creed of ignorance, the gospel of envy, its inherent virtue is the equal sharing of misery."

Socialism is ownership and control by the government of the means of production and of distribution. It is the stage following capitalism in the transition to communism. During this stage, according to Marxist theory, collectivism is implemented imperfectly. Communism is the ultimate utopia, a classless society run on the creed, "from each according to his ability, to each according to his need."

"Socius" is Latin for comrade and ally. You had to choose your comrades very carefully, lest you found yourself in jail or dead. "Communis" is Latin for "shared." I can attest first hand that nobody shared anything under communism except misery and poverty, except for the ruling elite. The communist "classless" society had two: the proletariat (the poor majority) and the ruling elite (rich communist party members).

The grandfather of all communists, Karl Marx, found a benefactor, Friedrich Engels, the son of a businessman in Prussia, to support him and his family while he sought re-distribution of wealth through "cultural and political revolution." Karl Marx was an intellectual bum who hated manual labor, finding ways with "ideas" to mooch off rich patrons.

While his large family survived on a diet of bread and potatoes, he worked on his "Communist Manifesto" with Engels. Three of his seven children died before the age of ten and one died in infancy because they were malnourished and literally starved to death.

In 1852, a police spy from Prussia said that Marx, with a Doctorate of Philosophy from Berlin University, "lived the life of a gypsy, rarely washing, combing, and changing his linens. He is a drunk and idle for days on end..." He was spied on as the leader of the Communist Party. Such philosophers as Marx were not interested in contributing anything productive in society, but destroying it and creating their communist Utopia. (Michael Savage)

Marx died a pauper, always living off inheritances, never holding any meaningful job to support his family. Espousing ideas and creating havoc in orderly society were more important to Marx than caring for his family or contributing to society in a positive way. His ideas laid the groundwork for immense destruction of property, of families, and the killing of millions of innocents across the globe.

The "creeping socialism" that Ronald Reagan, Dwight Eisenhower, and Friedrich von Hayek have warned us about has become blatant, daily reality: illegal government takeover of Chrysler, GM, student loan programs from banks, banking industry, health care, internet control, FCC radio programming content, stifling of conservative speech, attack on Christianity, its symbols, and Judeo-Christian values. The private sector is shrinking every day; our economy is becoming more and more socialist. "We are all socialists now," said Newsweek on its cover.

Having lived under socialism and communism for twenty years, I can attest that there is nothing "shared" except misery. There is nothing "equal" under communism except poverty; doctors, lawyers, mechanics, teachers were paid the same miserable salaries and had to work in less than desirable places, dictated by the communist party upon graduation. There is no "leveling of the playing field," to use the Democrat euphemism. There is no "economic security" but insecurity. There is no "living wage," another darling euphemism of the Democrats, but a barely surviving wage. The communist work ethic is, "we pretend to work, and they pretend to pay us."

Socialism and Communism are not open but repressive societies. There is no "universal healthcare," but rationing of it. There is no "public good, only the communist party "good" and goodies at specialized communist party-only stores. There is no free public education but forced indoctrination into the Marxist theory through Marxist Economics and the laughable "Scientific Socialism." Students of all ages had to study and pass these courses.

We define our civilization by our humanity. There was no humanity under communism. Life was worthless unless it was the life of those in power. If a baby was born with a fixable handicap, nobody bothered to spend valuable resources on repairing the problem, he/she was left to die unattended.

Students were vaccinated in school with the same 3-4 syringes and needles boiled in rusty pans every morning, not autoclaved. Hepatitis was rampant. Hospitals washed and re-washed bandages and cotton. Hospital personnel, from orderlies to nurses, to doctors had to be bribed in order to have proper care provided to the patient. Medical care and drugs were free but families had to provide sheets, towels, round the clock care, food, drugs bought on the black market. The patient who had no family to care for them lingered in a metal frame bed unattended for weeks until they got better on their own or died.

The doctor would write an order for a prescription and the hospital pharmacy could not fill it because they had run out of money allotted for the year to buy drugs. The family would buy the medicine on the black market and bring it to the hospital so it can be administered to the patient. When 4 p.m. came, everybody went home, nobody worked beyond the required 8 hours. Who cared if patients died during the night? There were no inquires and no accountability.

I have lost many family members to medical malpractice, lack of care, gross medical negligence, and rationing of care based on age or connections to the elite in power. "Death panels" were part of medical care. People lingered in hospitals for weeks, ignored by medical staff, untreated, unfed, literally screaming in pain, with no drugs available to ease the pain unless doctors were bribed with money, soap, shampoo, wine, food, cigarettes, gold, and foreign made goods.

We had free medical care for all in Romania but we did not get much. The doctors were poorly trained, had no adequate equipment, were under-paid, and violated the Hippocratic Oath daily by giving poor or no medical care unless bribes were given. Rationing was imposed in order to serve everybody. Ambulances were a joke – they came with no staff or emergency equipment and arrived not just hours but days late. Some drivers would stop on the way to the hospital to pick up hitchhikers in order to make extra money. The neglect and potholes were enough to kill anybody.

Pharmacy shelves were empty because the yearly allotted money for the area had run out. Americans have abundant drugs of any kind when they are sick. Can they picture the Black Market as the only choice at ten times the cost?

There is a reason why most Europeans have bad teeth; it is the result of socialized medicine. I had root canal as a teenager without anesthesia, blood spilling everywhere, screams of pain, while the doctor was spitting in my mouth talking to the nurse. After a few months of such torture, the tooth was pulled anyway. It is true, it did not cost me anything, but I got nothing in return but a lot of torture and pain.

Americans foolishly criticize doctors as greedy although they spend ten or more years in school and six figures in tuition. How many doctors would go into medicine if our government can now tell them how much they can earn and where they must practice medicine? Who is willing to invest the time and money when their salaries are going to equal those of a teacher who spends only $25,000 and four years in college?

Do you want to be treated by a mediocre medical student or the top of the class? Do you want to be treated by someone who graduated from a medical school in a third world country and came here on a work visa? There is a reason why doctors from third world nations cannot practice medicine in the U.S. unless they go to med school two more years and pass a licensing board – they are not trained properly by American medical standards. It is a known fact that those who can afford private treatment will come to the U.S. instead of accepting the free medical care in their countries. The wait alone and denial of services kill many people.

We have passed Obamacare in the dead of night, during the holidays, twisting arms, making back room deals, using obscene bribery, without lawmakers reading and debating such an important piece of legislation that affects one fifth of our economy, and now, we are finding out how disastrous it will be for our nation. It is so long and convoluted, it includes a 15-member board charged with rationing of care and many unrelated items such as taxes on sales of homes. It is not about healthcare, it is about total government control of the population.

Useful Idiots

During incipient communist regimes, the general population foolishly supported the wave of change that promised to fundamentally alter the balance of power and bring wealth and prosperity to the masses by expropriating and stealing from the "undeserving rich."

There is an argument to be made that some strata of society was exploited to the benefit of inherited wealth such as kings, queens, and large industrialist owners of sweatshops. However, some wealth was acquired through hard work, perseverance, wise investments, entrepreneurship, risk-taking, education, and luck; it was not "stolen" from anybody.

There is also an argument to be made that unions were beneficial in times such as those during Bismarck's reign in Germany or early nineteenth century Europe when unions negotiated sick leave, better working conditions, vacations, worker's compensation for injuries, and other benefits.

Economic conditions did not improve for the majority of the population; therefore, it was easy to believe that a new and improved regime, the socialists, would bring about positive "fundamental change" to people's lives.

Mismanagement of the economy is not something new, it is still practiced today in third world dictatorships and some European Union countries like Portugal, Italy, Greece, Ireland, and Spain who give lavish social benefits and welfare to their populations.

The Weimar Republic was the most glaring example of an economy in total disarray with hyperinflation so disastrous that it required a wheelbarrow of cash to buy a loaf of bread. It was easier to burn money in the fireplace than it was to purchase wood.

The immediate socialist supporters, teachers, professors, journalists, doctors, lawyers, active communist members of the inner circle were known as "useful idiots." They were "useful" as long as the few communists such as Lenin, Stalin, Castro, Mao were attempting to gain and garner control and power and their supporters willingly sacrificed their time, money, and loyalty.

Same groups became "idiots" when the communist leaders decided that total concentrated power into one man's hands was more desirable. Any immediate comrades became a threat to supreme leader's rule and necessitated their disposal. As the rest of the intellectuals realized they have been duped, they turned on their former leader. The dictator had no choice but to get rid of them.

Soon after taking total power over a socialist nation, the "gentle" former agitators and labor organizers became ruthless rulers who murdered millions, destroying the middle class. People wearing glasses were targeted and disposed of as intellectuals who posed a danger to the regime through their passionate knowledge and avid reading. Information was power. Innocent people who were not teachers, lawyers, engineers, but who had genetic eye defects and happened to wear glasses were rounded up as enemies of the state.

The November 2010 gave the American people the opportunity to voice their opinions in reference to the out-of-control spending, lending, printing, and devaluing of our currency that the Democrat-controlled Congress has engaged in the last two years.

It is painfully apparent that the 100 or so Republicans that were swept into power through the vote of "we the people" chose to ignore the voters' wishes.

The spending has not stopped, it has not even slowed down, and the Republican-controlled House appears to have no intention to make real cuts in spending or to pass a budget. Republicans are not addressing the Democrat-controlled Congress failure to pass a budget in three years. The compliant media is ignoring the issue entirely as if it does not exist while portraying the economy as booming. I understand stagflation, inflation with a stagnant economy.

Americans are feeling the high prices, high unemployment, and high-energy costs. The media can disingenuously say that we are in a recovery, reality demonstrates otherwise. The unemployment rate and inflation rate are purposefully underreported to deceive the public. Food and gasoline prices are not included in the calculation of the CPI, consumer price index.

It is beginning to look more and more as if we are the useful idiots who are inconvenient to our lawmakers' quest for power. The rallies, the faxes, the letters, the calls, the Tea Party protests were ignored. We were useful before and during the election. I am not saying that we are going to have the same fate as the "useful idiots" of the socialist regimes. But we are becoming the idiots that lawmakers are ignoring, making elections just an exercise in futility.

Taxpayers are treated more and more like unruly children who must be punished with new rules and regulations for disobeying. We are now the enemy of the "nanny state." What other steps can we take to remedy the situation before it is too late? When our currency is worth zero and will be replaced as the world's reserve currency, what will we do?

No Child Left Inside Act

On June 21, 2011, the Maryland State Board of Education proudly announced that students must be environmentally literate before they can graduate from high school. Each child must receive a comprehensive, multi-disciplinary environmental education aligned with the Maryland State Environmental Literacy Standards.

"This is a momentous day not only for Maryland but for educators across the country who are watching what Maryland does, and hoping to increase outdoor learning in their states," said Don Baugh, Director of the No Child Left Inside Coalition (NCLI).

Governor O'Malley said, "Only through exposure to nature and education about our fragile ecosystem can we create the next generation of stewards."

The sponsor of the No Child Left Inside Act was Congressman John Sarbanes. "No Child Left Inside will pave the way for a new era of environmental stewardship in this country." All co-sponsors of the bill were Democrats with the exception of the Susan Collins (R-ME) and Olympia Snowe (R-ME).

The No Child Left Inside Coalition is a "national partnership of over 2,000 business, health, youth, faith, recreational, environmental, and educational groups representing over 50 million Americans. The chapter in Maryland has over 225 group members, and represents over 635,000 Marylanders." The coalition list represents zoos, day camps, recreational parks, and national and international environmental groups.

No Child Left Inside is an environmentalist legislative effort pushed at the national and state levels to have pro environment, pro global warming and pro smart growth propaganda as a part of k-12 interdisciplinary education.

The sponsors of the bill claim, "studies show environmental education has a measurable, positive impact on student achievement not only in science but in math, reading, and social studies. Business leaders also increasingly believe an environmentally literate workforce is critical in a burgeoning green economy. We are very hard pressed to find this burgeoning green economy, it is mostly empty rhetoric.

"Field experiences and related activities, when part of the regular school curriculum in environmental education, also help students become healthier." I found a few College of Education lab experiments with a stated bias, as proof of this statement.

I discovered plenty of data showing the dismal state of education and schools in Maryland in math, science, and reading. Students can barely read, write, balance a checkbook, or solve simple math problems yet are now required to be stewards of the environment and explore it in depth across the curriculum.

Sarbanes believes that a more "holistic" approach to the curriculum is necessary. Somehow holistic does not mesh well with curriculum. It sounds like a College of Education new age, feel-good teaching method of the moment; let us throw $500 million in this "green" direction. We failed at teaching students to read, write, and compute, perhaps we can be successful at brainwashing them into believing that human activity is bad, causes global warming, and destroys the planet.

Apparently, environmental study and "green play" helps children cope with ADD and ease obesity rates. I thought proper nutrition, PE classes, competitive sports, and recess time where designed for physical exercise and thus weight control. What is "green play" anyway?

Proponents believe that environmental study helps with "nature deficit disorder." The term "nature-deficit disorder" was coined by author Richard Louv in his dramatically titled book, "Last Child in the Woods," to describe what happens to young people who become disconnected from their natural world. Richard Louv links lack of nature to some of the most disturbing childhood trends, such as the rise in obesity, attention disorders, and depression.

This reminds me of Rachel Carson's book, "Silent Spring," who claimed that DDT killed all the birds, hence the title. Her book started the environmental movement in the U.S. DDT was banned for agricultural use in most developed countries in 1968. Three million people around the globe die unnecessarily each year of mosquito-induced malaria. DDT was controlling the spread of mosquitoes.

No Child Left Inside Act gives "American students the knowledge that they will need to make informed personal decisions and act as responsible citizens as they face environmental challenges that previous generations never imagined." This is UN Agenda 21

Armageddon scare tactics to frighten Americans into global compliance to its goals of severely limiting the use of water, electricity, transportation, and denial of human access to wilderness areas all in the name of nature conservation and environmental stewardship.

Americans have been stewards of our environment for generations and resolved issues without any special interdisciplinary curriculum indoctrination from k-12 grades. What are the environmental challenges that previous generations never imagined? This is a very important question for the Maryland curriculum writers.

No Child Left Inside Act claims, "environmental education also promotes higher-order thinking skills and is correlated with higher test scores in math and reading." There is no such evidence and no way to prove that higher test scores are actually connected to environmentalism.

The statement, "Environmental Education is the foundation for creating the green workforce of the new economy," is a shameless intent of this new curriculum to brainwash our children into the Global Management System (GMS), a world-wide blue print for international totalitarian control of earth and resources, including human resources, under the fuzzy excuses that children are fat, need play time outdoors, and re-connect with nature while their ADD is being soothed. Where are the **green workforce** and **the new economy**? Is this another example of non-existent shovel-ready jobs?

Here is a short list of National coalition members who supported the No Child Left Inside Act in Maryland:
- Adventure Treks
- African American Environmentalist Association
- Alliance for Climate Education
- Alliance for Community Trees
- American Camp Association
- American Canoe Association
- American Cave Conservation Association
- American Deer & Wildlife Alliance
- American Forest Foundation
- American Horticultural Society
- American Recreation Coalition
- American Rivers
- American Sail Training Association
- American Society of Landscape Architects
- American Sports fishing Association
- American Trails

- o Biosphere Foundation
- o The Early Development of Global Education
- o Earth Day Network
- o Earth Force, Inc.
- o Forest Service Hispanic Employees Association
- o Global Green USA
- o Global Youth Leadership Institute
- o Greening Youth Foundation
- o National Hispanic Environmental Council
- o National Project for Excellence in Environmental Education
- o Sierra Club
- o World Forestry Center

Here is a short list of International supporters of the No Child Left Inside Act in Maryland:

- o African Volunteer Football Academy for the Less privileged (AVFAL) (Cameroon)
- o Assiniboine Park Conservancy (Canada)
- o Patgiri (India)
- o Istituto Pangea Onlus (Italy)
- o Citizenship Leadership Training Centre (Nigeria)
- o Equilibri Naturali
- o NOTL Sustainability Network

NOTL Sustainability Network (Green Feet People) is a "non-profit community environmental organization whose mandate is "greening NOTL one step at a time". This includes promoting the **sustainability** of the housing sector, food systems, energy, water and materials consumption, education, transportation and health." This is one of the thousands of ICLEI (International Council for Local Environmental Initiatives) local chapters in our cities and counties, which are tasked with **"smart growth"** to usurp property rights and Constitutional rights. They persuade local officials to revise zoning laws to fit into a "smart code zoning template." As a result, a massive reshuffling of property rights takes place.

UNEP (United Nations Environment Programme) prepared a Global Biodiversity Assessment of the state of the planet in order to validate Global Management System (GMS) by using doomsday predictions:

- Population reduction

- Oppressive lifestyle regulations
- Coercive return to earth-centered religions
- Self-sustaining human settlements

"Environmental education provides critical tools for a 21st century workforce," says the No Child Left Inside Act. UN Agenda 21 is the global contract of the 21st century between the 179 nations that participated in the 1992 Rio de Janeiro conference. United Nations with its many umbrella organizations plan to change the way we live, eat, earn, learn, and communicate under the aegis of "Save the Earth."

"The vast majority of Americans are convinced that the environment will become at least one of the dominant issues and challenges of the 21st century, as the growing needs of the growing global population increasingly presses up against the limits of the earth's resources and ecosystems." This is a Malthusian prediction that has population reduction and control written all over it.

Charles O. Holliday, Jr., Chairman and CEO of DuPont, declared that "an environmentally sustainable business is just good business, given the growing concern for environmental problems across America. A key component of an environmentally sustainable business is a highly educated work force, particularly involving environmental principles."

Author of "Walk the Talk- the Business Case for Sustainable Development," Charles O. Holliday, Jr. is a member/leader of the "U.S. Council on Competitiveness." This Orwellian leftist organization prizes government/private sector "collaboration." Its website congratulates Obama for his legislative accomplishments in the manufacturing arena. If you count all the jobs that have been shipped overseas during his administration, he has been quite successful in improving the lives of citizens in other countries.

It is true that children today spend many hours in front of a computer or television set. No parent would object to field trips or caring for the environment. Nobody wants his or her children to be obese. However, forcing a federal law that would spread across the land, indoctrinating children into environmental stewardship smacks eerily of global Marxism.

Parents have no problem with their children getting out of the classroom for field trips, to learn about ecology, recycling, nature preservation, and biology. If the state forces, advocates, or brainwashes students to believe that humans are evil, that we should not drive cars, live on private property, reproduce, and that we have caused global warming, that is UN Agenda 21 propaganda.

Encounter with "Occupy Wall Street" in D.C.

Walking down Pennsylvania Avenue on a blistery day, I encountered one of the makeshift squalid camps of Occupy D.C. The colorful and dingy tents were empty. A few homeless people were milling about waiting for capitalist lunch delivery to the camp. They would have had to wait a long time under communism to have anything delivered free. If you did not work, you did not get food or shelter.

Environmentalists, anarchists, and communists want to live in filth, squalor, with no electricity, no water, and no sewage, all in the name of saving the planet. These occupiers are ideal useful idiots to the communist movement sponsored and funded by labor unions and community activists with socialist agendas.

The crudely hand-lettered cardboard signs read, "Welcome to Occupywashingtondc.org," "Job, Schools, Healthcare Are a Right," "Party for Socialism and Liberation," "Billionaires your time is up," (PSLweb.org) "Keep your promise, British Petroleum, make us whole," "MOVE OVER AIPAC! Time for real democracy in the Middle East! Global Exchange" (moveoveraipac.org). For graphic impact, someone had drawn a very large fish swallowing a tiny one. To make sure that nobody misunderstood how Marxist these campers were, the signs were done in vivid red.

No need to explain that the PSL (Party for Socialism and Liberation) are the American Marxists and moveoveraipac.org are supporters of the non-existent state of Palestine, supporters of the so-called Arab Spring (the take-over of the Muslim Brotherhood of the Middle East), and supporters of Iran (the state that wants to wipe the state of Israel off the map with nukes).

The second Occupy D.C. camp was located in McPherson Square. General James Birdseye McPherson must be rolling in his grave about now, terribly unhappy with what these malcontent anarchists and squatters have done to our beautiful capital and its parks.

On the 41 day of "occupation," the Washington Post dedicated two full pages and a half to this Big Labor supported and funded anarchy, under the whimsical title, "A Square Gets Hip." The fact that the National Park Service is allowing them to set up a continuous elaborate camp on public property indefinitely is a mystery in itself.

Although "camping is not officially permitted," officers are asking "visitors" to move their tents every four days to prevent damage to the turf. Since the whole area is covered with tents, it seems like an exercise in futility. Keeping soft drinks away from the stonework of Gen. McPherson's statue is encouraged. "Littering and public urination are prohibited."

When the tea party had a one-day event in the same square, they had to clear the premises before 6 p.m. They had to obtain numerous permits and were not allowed to set up any tents or start the event before a certain time. Attendees were not permitted to stand on sidewalks and police presence was heavy.

The tea party in Richmond, Virginia paid fees in the neighborhood of $8,000 in order to hold an event yet the squatters of Occupy Richmond are charged nothing. A lawsuit by the tea party group was underway to recoup their money.

The Washington Post writer called "Camp Malcolm" of Occupy D.C., improvised "vibrant urbanism, an aesthetic and cultural phenomenon, rooted in pedigrees in the world of art and architecture." He continued his lofty praise of these young malcontent communists as pioneers in "a living exercise in do-it-yourself urbanism, a trendy movement that strives to engage ordinary people in a hands-on approach to shaping and claiming public space."

They trashed our beautiful public park and capital with tents, teepees, and destroyed the turf. They used AFL-CIO showers down the street, two SEIU donated port-o-potties, donated food, donated books, donated money and clothing, public water, public resources for cleaning and extra police protection paid by taxpayer money and yet wanted to live simply. Who is going to pay for and subsidize their "simple living?"

The concrete walkways through the park have been renamed Gandhi Avenue, Che Guevara Avenue, Angela Davis Avenue, Malcolm X Avenue, and Harvey Milk Blvd., leaving no doubt about their communist ideology and intentions to "fundamentally change" our republic into a communist regime. Only Marxists would idolize Che Guevara, who contributed to the death and murder of thousands of innocents.

Good ole capitalist Starbucks provided the camp with day-old pastries, Wi-Fi, and restrooms before the portable johns arrived. Who knew that anarchists, who want to live so simply off the work of others, need Internet connection and electronic gadgets in order to exist in their workers' paradise under total government control?

The occupiers were highly organized; they printed two papers in an attempt to spread their propaganda. They must have slept in history classes because totalitarian societies do not allow any printing, writing, public speaking, public meetings, or expression of ideas without the permission and approval of the communist party.

According to the Washington Post, the occupiers' health was manned by someone "certified in CPR and automated-defibrillator use, who took a semester-long course in wilderness first aid in college." Doctors and nurses trained by the western, "evil" capitalist system, volunteered on Wednesdays. Clean water was provided by taxpayer water fountains. The hypocrisy of these mooching individuals, demanding free goods and services produced by the hard labor of real capitalist Americans, was galling.

Seeking to "disrupt daily life in creative ways" was the "lofty" goal of these pathetic individuals because they believed that under "neoliberalism, we can all throw a pie in the face of economic fascism." But "economic fascism" better feed them, house them, pay their college loans, give them jobs, vacations, care for their kids, give them cars, gasoline, and health care. All they have to do is show up, create mayhem, and squat camp in the middle of a busy city. After all, "it is truly applied aesthetics."

In their madness, these moochers want to organize people around basic needs such as food and healthcare, and "blur the lines between public and private space." I personally love an organized society and do not wish to live in anarchy, begging for food, medical care, clothes, and shelter. I am proud to own a home for which I have worked honestly. I enjoy having my private, quiet space, my kitchen, and the ability to feed, clothe, and shelter my family. I do not wish my reality to be ruled by the poetic idealism and ignorance of drugged hippies, who do not like formal organization, despise work, law, and order.

Trying to legitimize squatting in the middle of a busy city, the Washington Post article compares occupiers with camps set up by the Romans and New Orleans after Katrina. Romans were highly organized and their camps were a symbol of order and civilized society. They were forced to do so while away from Rome during military campaigns. A natural disaster hardly compares with fifty or so malcontents who squat during the day in the middle of a busy city while going home at night to the expensive suburban homes of their parents.

As the author declared McPherson Square "Washington's most vibrant public square," I was reminded that these misguided youth turned violent last week. They kept many conservative conference attendees hostage downtown D.C. by blocking all access roads and the exits from the building with their bodies while the police watched.

The anti-Americanism flowing through the camp taught them that it was acceptable to push elderly women and a handicapped person down the stairs, injuring them in the process. The end justifies the means. Numerous videos surfaced on the web, attesting to their violence. This was no longer a peaceful, disorganized protest, it was violent, focused, and anti-American. Their occupation must end. Hard working Americans want their cities back from these societal vagrants.

Pushing Back the Socialist Agenda in Education

As the Americans' indifference to the destruction of our country intensified, the indoctrination and brainwashing from the left of our citizens and of their children accelerated.

I watched during Thanksgiving a National Geographic special on the pilgrims landing at Jamestown, Virginia. The strong environmentalist language shocked me.

Claiming that Europeans completely deforested the land, overfished to the point of emptying the lakes and rivers and causing a severe reduction of the teaming fish population, and of their size, was outrageous. Impressionable minds, who hear such broad, sweeping statements, are mislead by design because no scientific data or evidence is offered to support these claims.

The video continued that Europeans have brought with them seeds of wheat and grain weeds such as dandelion, thus causing "biological imperialism." If wind carries seeds of plants and weeds over large swaths of land in the natural process of plant life, is it still called "biological imperialism?"

These ridiculous statements fall in line with the environmental agenda of "man as the destroyer of the planet." The earth is in danger because man has caused global warming and only by destroying our economic system, drastically reducing human population, and returning to a primitive lifestyle would assure the survival of the globe.

I can see how frightening these made-up scenarios could be to an innocent young mind or the uninformed. Virginia is covered with beautiful lush forests. Areas where wood was harvested are restocked with seedlings for many reasons. Soil erosion prevention is one such important component of forest replacement.

As my children were growing up, Channel One News was part of their curriculum on a daily basis. Budding television stars on the left side of the political spectrum indoctrinated students on issues dear to the heart of the left. Most parents had no idea that their children received such a one-sided view of the world but I knew. Having lived under communism, I could recognize all the platitudes, empty promises, lies, and slogans.

Perusing Channel One News recently, I found many educational, environmental, and political videos and links. One video touted National Hispanic Heritage Month, September 15-October 15, in honor of the anniversaries of independence of Chile, Costa Rica, El Salvador, Belize, Guatemala, Honduras, Nicaragua, and Mexico. Who knew that celebrating the anniversaries of independence of South American countries was so important that we had to have a National Hispanic Heritage Month? As the video says, the face of America is changing and diversity is paramount. This was contradicting our country's founding principles of "unity." The leftist immigration policies emphasize "diversity."

Under Teaching Tools, there were lesson plans on history, sociology, and environmentalism: The History of Thanksgiving, The History of Hate, Our Disposable Lives, Mexican Drug Cartels, and The Haves and Have-Nots. The seeds of class envy, class warfare, bigotry, and hate were planted solidly in these videos. Disliking something or disagreeing with someone was presented as hate.

Revolution Earth was highlighting the Nature Conservancy with its Leaders for Environmental Action for the Future (LEAF) internships slated for environmental careers in green transportation solutions, protecting and caring for the environment. The video stated that such fields earn 25% more than non-environmental careers and the environmental green job field is growing three times as much as other jobs. Twisting the facts was bad enough. No mention was made of all the bankruptcies of alternative energy companies who have squandered billions of taxpayer dollars or the faux "green jobs."

Videos on bio fuels, electric cars, going green, pollution cruise, green holiday shopping, oil spills, and the proverbial polar bears in danger completed the environmental indoctrination and brainwashing. No mention that polar bears are very good swimmers, do not usually drown, and have multiplied five times in numbers.

A whole section was dedicated to Islam and the Ground Zero mosque but no mention was made of the Christian persecution in the Middle East, deliberate destruction of churches by intolerant Islamic ideology, and all the killings and torture of innocent Christians.

A video dedicated to the "growing white Nazi hate groups," exaggerated the numbers and the influence they have, and painted them as the Americans on the border fighting illegal immigration, making the disingenuous inference that those who oppose illegal immigration and want the laws of the land enforced are haters.

Frank had a very interesting comment about illegal immigration. "You catch a burglar in YOUR house who insists that you built YOUR house FOR HIM. He demands that you move out to make room for him and all his friends and relatives. If you refuse to do this, you are a racist, bigot, homophobe, intolerant hate-monger, and whatever else the usurper can think of to intimidate you into surrendering your birthright to him. He calls this social plunder "redistribution of wealth," and "social justice." I quoted Frank because this is exactly the mentality inculcated into our children's minds by the educational establishment.

Home schooling is gaining track with many parents who want to avoid their children's socialist indoctrination in public schools. As Christopher Wright found out, Georgetown Law Center Professor, Robin L. West, made curious, fallacious, and uninformed arguments against home schooling.

- "Most home schooled children have fundamentalist Protestant parents who teach their   kids 'nothing but the Bible
- Homeschooled children are at higher risk for child abuse
- Other harms justify strict regulation of homeschooling including curriculum reviews and invasive home visits"
- It was a crime to keep children home from school until 30 years ago"

Our Founding Fathers did not attend public schools yet they were brilliant. Students did quite well prior to 1979 when the Department of Education was established. Statistical data show that the level of education and student performance have decreased since 1979.

Homeschooled children represented every demographic imaginable – pagans, atheists, lower income, upper income, conservative, liberal, Ph.D.'s, GED's. Doctoral student Jeremy E. Uecker from the University of Texas conducted a nationwide phone survey in 2008 and "found very little effect of homeschooling on any aspect of adolescents' religious views." "Only 17 percent of suspected abuse reports are submitted by education personnel."(Christopher Wright)

Public school advocates, educational lefties, academics, and Marxists wanted "social engineering" of our children's minds, as Dewey wrote, "social reconstruction," well known in the circles of communism.

Textbooks are generally written by college professors to slant history in the direction of the leftist view with total disregard for historical accuracy. An effort by the Prince William County Tea Party is underway in the State of Virginia to review all textbooks for accuracy of content. There are 11 states across the country that either have completed or are doing textbook reviews.

"Our Living Constitution Then and Now," a textbook used for grades 5-8 in American History classes, teaches our children that "Rights are special privileges **the government gives you**. You are also **given the right to choose a religion**." The government does not give you a right; you have a God-given right. "The Bill of Rights lists the freedoms given to citizens." Actually, the Bill of Rights lists the freedoms granted by the Constitution. "Because **the government gives us rights**, we have the duty to be good citizens. But what does it mean to be a good citizen? How can you be a part of **giving back for the freedom you have?**" The government does not give us rights and we are not required to give back restitution for our rights. The fallacies and falsehoods in this book alone were shocking.

"On July 14, 2005, Governor Pawlenty signed the 128 page Minnesota Omnibus Bill into law called The American Heritage in Public Education Act. Included are two important paragraphs that encouraged schools to teach America's Founding Principles from original sources and prevent the censorship of religious reference from those sources. Teachers can now introduce their students to America's uncensored Judeo-Christian heritage without fear." (edwatch.org)

In a Virginia High School AP History Class, students were forbidden to use any outside help/reference/access to information or opinion for their work under the threat of disciplinary action and a failing grade. The students could not even discuss their assignments with their parents. Parent Amy Fuentes was shocked. The Westfield High School's explanation was that the move was intended to create a level-playing field for all students because some did not have access to information. I found this hard to believe since most classrooms have computers; their libraries have computers, encyclopedias, and other reference sources. Furthermore, Fairfax County is one of the richest counties in the nation. Students were not allowed to discuss ideas, opinions, or ask questions of anybody but the teacher. This was an obvious attempt to control what students thought, allowing only the teacher's point of view and that of the textbook writers.

Delegate Rich Anderson, R-Woodbridge, leads the State Commission on Civics in Education. The purpose of the commission is "to educate students on the importance of citizen involvement in a representative democracy, the promotion of the study of state and local government among the commonwealth citizenry, and the enhancement of communication and collaboration among organizations in the commonwealth that conduct civics education programs."

Adam Schaeffer, policy analyst with the Cato Center for Educational Freedom, argued in "The Public Education Tax Credit" that "Educational freedom can most effectively be realized through nonrefundable education tax credits – for both parents' education costs for their own children and taxpayer donations to nonprofit scholarship funds; tax credits enjoy practical, legal, and political advantages over school vouchers."

Schaeffer says, "Vouchers are grants of government funds, while tax credits are private funds." The U.S. Supreme Court ruling in Arizona Christian School Tuition Organization v. Winn made the distinction clear.

Colorado stopped its voucher program because of a state constitutional provision that did not allow charitable, educational, industrial, or benevolent appropriations to any person, corporation, or community under the absolute control of the state. Pennsylvania had a similar provision with exception for higher education.

American parents have begun to push back the socialist agenda and the public school indoctrination that their children have been subjected to for the past 50 years. This indoctrination bore fruit in the anarchic societal and economic confusion of the Occupy Wall Street denizens.

The New Renaissance in Education (NRIE) promotes "a curriculum to teach America's heritage to the next generation: liberty and limited government, America's documents, America's cultural heritage, free market economics, and western intellectual tradition." This worthy educational program should spread across the nation with the help of dedicated parents, teachers, and freedom loving Americans.

Reformulating "No Child Left Behind Act" the Pelosi Way

Congress passed in 1965 the Elementary and Secondary Education Act (ESEA), which provided federal funding for K-12 education. The ESEA encompasses Title I, the federal government's flagship aid program for disadvantaged students. The ESEA has been renewed eight times, most recently by the No Child Left Behind Act (NCLB). The NCLB Act of 2001 was signed into law by President Bush on January 8, 2002.

The No Child Left Behind Act was intended to push student achievement by holding states and schools accountable for student progress. The bill appeared well intentioned; however, it was an attempt to transform education by government control without holding parents accountable for their children's educational progress at all.

Six areas were emphasized in the No Child Left Behind Act:

1. **Annual Testing**: Students in grades 3-8 were to begin testing by 2005-06 school year in reading and mathematics. Testing in science had to be done beginning with 2007-08 school year at least once in elementary, middle, and high school. Schools and teachers designed the curriculum so that most of the teaching was tailored to test taking and not to long-term retention of knowledge.
2. **Academic Progress:** States had to bring all students up to the "proficient" level on state tests by the 2013-14 school year. A formula in the law required certain schools to meet state "adequate yearly progress" for all students and certain demographic groups.

   Title I funding schools who failed the educational targets two years in a row would receive assistance and students could attend other public schools. If such schools failed three years in a row, private tutoring was offered. Schools with constant failures to meet targets would be subjected to leadership change.

3. **Report Cards:** States and school districts were required to show student-achievement data broken down by subgroups and school-by-school, starting with 2002-2003 school year.

4. **Teacher Qualifications:** By the end of the 2005-06 school year, every public school teacher in core content areas had to be "highly qualified" in the subject he/she taught. "Highly qualified" meant that a teacher was licensed and demonstrably proficient in his/her subject matter.

   Most teachers were College of Education graduates who performed poorly on the National Teacher Exam. Certification was not difficult to obtain for a College of Education graduate.

   Certification, varying from state to state, was a very complex and time-consuming process for graduates with College of Arts and Science degrees. A teacher with advanced degrees from a College of Arts and Science could not teach in public schools without mandatory certification. The best and brightest graduates with degrees in fields such as math, science, Foreign Languages, English, history could teach college but not public school students. Teacher unions were very protective of their College of Education graduates to the detriment of our children.

5. **Reading First:** "The act created a new competitive-grant program called Reading First, funded at $1.02 billion in 2004, to help states and districts set up "scientific, research-based" reading programs for children in grades K-3 (with priority given to high-poverty areas). A smaller early-reading program sought to help states better prepare 3- to 5-year-olds in disadvantaged areas to read. The program's funding was later cut drastically by Congress amid budget talks." (Education Week)

6. **Funding Changes:** By altering the Title I funding formula, the No Child Left Behind Act (NCLB) targeted resources to school districts with high concentrations of poor children. The NCLB had provisions to give states and districts more flexibility in how they spent part of their federal money.

On October 19, 2011, the Senate began the markup of Senator Tom Harkin's (D-CA) 860-page proposal to revamp and rewrite the Elementary and Secondary Education Act (ESEA). His strategy was the same as Nancy Pelosi's strategy for Obamacare, "you will have to pass the bill so you can find out what is in it."

The proposal had new regulations added to already burdened school districts with the goal of maintaining and increasing the current Department of Education control of public education. The Senate has not had time to read the bill nor had it received input from those whom it seeks to control.

Senator Rand Paul said, "The bill is 860 pages and we got it yesterday, and I talked to committee members today and said this isn't the way government should work. I thought we'd have hearings. We've had zero hearings on No Child Left Behind. I would think we'd have several significant hearings...Bring in the teachers, bring in the superintendents, bring in the principals and find out more about it. We've had none of that, and I think it's rotten."

Senator Rand Paul introduced 100 amendments, including a complete repeal of NCLB, in order to slow down the committee and force them to take time to consider everything in Harkin's proposal.

School districts were already screaming for freedom from the federal red tape of NCLB, wanting their decision-making authority back. States should have been allowed to opt out of the No Child Left Behind and to spend dollars specifically to meet their needs. Federal control has not worked in the past, as evidenced by poor student performance and test scores.

Another bill crafted behind closed doors, the Harkin proposal placed emphasis on "equitable distribution" of teachers among schools and replaced existing federal standards with requirements that states prove they have "college- and career-ready" standards, giving the Department of Education in Washington, D.C. more control over the content taught in local schools.

Americans thought public school textbooks contained too much revisionist history. Wait until the Obama education team takes control of textbook contents now. States who want and need Title I funds must jump through the hoops of the "Obama Administration's new Common Core standards," all 860 pages drafted behind closed doors. (Heritage Foundation)

New Norm in Obama Regime: Graduates who Can't Read

The goal of the 2001 No Child Left Behind Act was to have every student proficient in reading and mathematics by 2014. Proposed by George W. Bush shortly after he took office, the bill had bipartisan support in Congress. The Act required states to develop assessments in basic skills for all students in certain grades in order for states to receive federal funding.

State and local education officials have been asking federal government authorities for relief from their own student testing mandates because more and more schools have been labeled failures due to less and less students passing the reading standards during each spring testing.

"Critics say the goals are unrealistic and brand schools as failures even if they make progress."

Schools are closed and teachers are fired because of these "unrealistic reading testing goals." It is shocking that being able to read and interpret simple paragraphs in English is considered unrealistic. Could it be because progressive teachers are more interested in lumping American kids with illegal alien students in ESL Science class? Why do we teach Science to American students in an ESL class? How much money is that costing the U.S. taxpayers?

Obama administration is coming to the rescue by exempting schools from the federal law's testing mandate. Problem solved, let us dumb down American education even further and give the "poor overworked" teachers and students a waiver. Let us fix the lowest performing schools by lowering the standards even more.

Arne Duncan, the Education Secretary, announced on August 8, 2011 a waiver to all 50 states with more details coming out in September. "Nothing in this plan for temporary relief from some aspects of the federal law will undermine what Congress is still discussing in terms of revising federal education laws," said Duncan.

The temporary relief was the federal funding that schools need to operate in the current school year in order to graduate more students who cannot read well or pass basic standards, as they should, in accordance with the No Child Left Behind Act.

"Duncan has warned that 82 percent of U.S. schools could be labeled failures next year if No Child Left Behind is not changed." Apparently, schools are not afraid to meet the standards but need more time and the freedom to institute change at their own pace. Principals claim that they need more flexibility and time. Just how long does a student need to learn to read English and to do basic math? Are thirteen years not enough time?

Montana Schools Superintendent Denise Juneau said, "her state isn't afraid of high standards and education reform but needs enough time to reach those standards and freedom to institute change in a way that works for Montana."

Could it be that schools and teachers spend too much time on alternative learning methodology, too many ESL classes, bilingual curriculum, multicultural curriculum, unnecessary electives, environmental literacy curriculum, revisionist history, and non-academic topics?

Many elementary schools pay Spanish translators after school to teach illegal immigrants' children how to do basic math and reading skills. These children speak Spanish only in their homes. When they test with English speaking students, their poor scores bring down the overall scores for that class and the school in general.

Billions of dollars are spent annually on bilingual and multicultural programs at the expense of reading and basic mathematics. Nobody knows for sure the exact amount since it is not just the Department of Education that engages in such practices.

Representative Virginia Foxx (R-NC) introduced H.R. 1715, the Multilingual Services Accounting Act. This bill required "the Department of Education and every government agency to create a new section in their annual accountability report that details any cost associated with providing multilingual services, such as verbal, written, or other services in languages other than English."

H.R. 1715 defined "fees paid for translators for non-English speakers, the cost for private contractors' employees to learn languages other than English, the cost of preparing, translating, printing, or recording of documents, records, Web sites, brochures, pamphlets, flyers, or other materials in a language other than English."

H.R. 1715 is self-executing. If the bill will pass, the Director of the Office of Management and Budget would have six months to inform every government agency CFO to provide all of the multilingual services accounting information required under section 902(a)(6)(E) of H.R. 1715. The bill is still in committee and has a 1 percent chance of passing.

H.R. 1715 could have provided the badly needed accountability that schools and other government agencies owe to the American people. The hard-working taxpayers need to know how their money is wasted on a dumbed-down, multicultural education that appeases leftist political correctness.

Common Core and Universal Design for Learning

I was having a cup of inflation-stricken chili that looked a few ounces smaller than before – the Michelle food-police with her holier-than-thou dictates of nutrition must have convinced the owners of the chain to change portion size while increasing the price.

I became privy to the loud conversation of three young women in their early twenties from the nearby table. One was bemoaning the lack of a raise in three years to her $44,000 a year teaching job – she had had enough and was going to look for another job. I was wondering if anybody sent her the memo that 25 percent of college graduates in her age group, 25 and younger, are unemployed and would gladly take her job.

High school teaching and a library science degree were the source of their displeasure and the list was quite long. Who decided that filing books in a library by the Dewey system is a science?

Dealing with a liberal education curriculum, demanding administrators, unruly students who challenge any authority and come unprepared to school every day, placating helicopter parents who hover at school all day, objecting to anything American, demanding progressivism, multiculturalism in teaching methodology, or parents who only care if their children have three free meals a day away from home, can be challenging. Complicating the problem is the lack of subject matter knowledge of some teachers and the political correctness required in the classroom. All can make someone's life quite miserable at work.

Making only $44,000 in early twenties is certainly an outrage for young people in the Obama-entitled society. After all, they were promised a six-figure salary by their college advisor and plenty of jobs in spite of their unemployable field of study. Such overt "social injustice" can only be rectified by confiscating wealth from the rich and distributing it to the young. It is a right now to have everything that someone else has, regardless of effort or age. Why wait and build up a career and experience when you can demand full rights here and now?

You can always take to the streets with the Occupiers and burn American flags, deface buildings, cars, and squat in the middle of a busy city or a beautiful park to make your demands known. If you are a nuisance to the taxpayers who must dodge your flea-infested camp daily on their way to work while they can no longer use the park they are paying for, and you cause millions of dollars in public property damage, so be it, America is rich and can afford it.

We no longer teach a common culture, common identity, common true history, or values such as hard work, charity, morals, virtue, and the rule of law. The new freedom among the youth is anarchy. Secular education and "green" environmentalism in support of mother earth has become the new religion.

Greek universities are offering protection to the young anarchists and rioters. If they make it to campuses, the police cannot arrest them without a warrant from the university presidents who, of course, refuse to issue them. Education is encouraging anarchy and lawlessness in Greece.

Goethe, a classical liberal, warned us that democracy is incompatible with liberty. "Legislators and revolutionaries who promise equality and liberty at the same time are psychopaths." Political centralization would lead to the destruction of culture. (Hans Hermann Hoppe, Ludwig von Mises Institute)

Common Core national standards, another President Obama brainchild, will implement among schools a Race to the Top competition through federal grants. If states adopt his Common Core standards, they will be exempt from the onerous provisions of No Child Left Behind (NCLB) mandates.

According to the Brookings Institution, "The empirical evidence suggests that the Common Core will have little effect on American students' achievement. The nation will have to look elsewhere for ways to improve its schools."

The authority to create and set standards belongs to states and school districts, not the federal government. Better yet, parents should have the power to give their children the type of education that best suits their children's needs and abilities.

The Department of Education does not know best – it paid two Washington, D.C. organizations, the National Governors Association's Center for Best Practices and The Council of Chief State School

Officers, to come up with the Common Core national standards. (Pioneer Institute)

According to Lance Izumi, author of "Obama's Education Takeover," the President "strong-armed the states into adopting these standards through a number of devices, principally through the Race to the Top competition through federal grants."

Awards in Race to the Top $4 billion "historic" grant scheme will go to states "leading coherent, compelling, and comprehensive education reform." It was authorized under the American Recovery and Reinvestment Act of 2009.

"Assessments have to be developed that are valid, support and inform instruction, provide accurate information about what students know and can do, and measure student achievement against standards designed to ensure that all students gain the knowledge and skills needed to succeed in college and the workplace." (Race to the Top)

My translation is, dilute education, water down curriculum, force everybody into one "successful mold," and receive an undeserved pass, a high school diploma and a worthless college degree. Exceptionalism is discouraged; poor students are rewarded, while achievers are punished.

In my 30 years experience as a teacher, the College of Education came up with many experimental programs that promised to be a breakthrough in education and ended up as another giant waste of taxpayer dollars.

"As the nation seeks to maintain our international competitiveness, ensure all students, regardless of background, have access to a high quality education, and prepare all students for college, work and citizenship, these standards are an important foundation for our *collective* work." (Arne Duncan on Core Standards)

Searching deeper into the Core Standards, the true intent is clear, "all children can and should learn to high achievement standards." Policymakers must "endorse, fund, and recognize *assessment regimes* that accomplish this goal," *Universal Design* and *Universal Design for Learning*. Really? All children can learn to high achievement standards? Our minds, IQs, learning styles, and God-given talents are so equal now that everything is possible by government fiat?

Apparently, standardized tests "fail to produce a valid and reliable measurement of what significant minorities of students actually know, especially students with disabilities, English language learners or those from varied cultural backgrounds. Without accurate measurement, accountability systems are not only ineffective, they are *unethical.*" (Core Standards)

It will be a fascistic world in which every person will be forced into a government-dictated and enforced, dumbed-down mold, where everybody is equally intelligent, equally capable, equally trained, equally able, and equally educated with a diploma on the wall that is not worth the paper with the fancy intaglio printing.

Now What? Unionized College Professors?

I never liked reading the Washington Post because it is exclusively a leftist paper. However, there are views that are important to ponder in order to stay informed of the disastrous direction our country is being forced towards by a minority of Americans who lust to live in socialist Europe. I wonder why the left "suffers" in our "socially unjust" country when we would gladly buy them a one-way ticket to the communist paradise of their choice.

A Saturday column, "A better professor, thanks to the union," irritated me because it was full of misrepresentations and distortions of truth. The author, Bob Lehrman, may truly believe his hypothesis. I am irritated because the left is trying to regulate and control every aspect of our daily lives, including education.

Lehrman advocates that adjunct professors should join a union such as SEIU because their membership would strengthen colleges. SEIU organizes labor in three sectors: health care, public service, and property services.

I am not sure membership in SEIU would strengthen any college, but I am sure that guaranteed employment would turn faculty into phantom tenured professors. It is rare that the professor of record ever shows up for his or her class, they are too busy writing for publication, conferencing, writing grants, or giving speeches to like-minded leftists to be bothered with teaching. Tenured "teaching" is relegated to graduate teaching assistants who try their best to explain difficult material that is often over their heads.

As a former academic, I have met plenty high school faculty who were union members and college professors who were very poor teachers. Once tenured, it is nearly impossible to get rid of a teacher or a professor, no matter how dismal his/her performance is in the classroom. That is if they are in the classroom at all. They are busy making the lecture circuit, the conference circuit, and research for research's sake circuit. They are the advertised professor of record but a lowly graduate teaching assistant with little supervision is the de facto teacher. Often they do not speak English very well because they come from China, India, Pakistan, or other such far-away places. They have no training but try very hard. The department head is obligated to give them classes to teach because the deans have already hired them and cannot rescind the assistantship because it comes hand in hand with their graduate school attendance in fields that most Americans eschew like mathematics, chemistry, and physics.

American students who pay very high tuition for top-notch education are frustrated by their inability to understand the lectures and their instructor's thick accents. How is that a better college?

Lehrman believes that Adjunct Professors are treated unfairly since they have no offices, no benefits, few perks, and are fired at a moment's notice. "They need a union."

I have been an adjunct for 25 years and never understood that it was anything else but a temporary, part-time job that I chose to do in addition to my full load at a different university. I did not need benefits, I did not expect them, and I did not demand them. I do not think any private sector part-time jobs offer any perks or special treatment. I signed my contract each semester, agreed to the pay, and joyfully taught my adjunct classes.

I never had a union represent me when I signed my yearly contract for my full-time teaching job. I knew my expertise and the outstanding teaching job and excellent results were enough reflection of my ability and a passport to a new contract every year. We accepted the negotiated contract by the state according to our years of experience and education. I was an indispensable part of the organization. When I retired, four part-time teachers were hired to replace me because none of them could do alone what I did and was educated to do.

Bob Lehrman thinks that a "unionized workforce can make teachers better." Standardized tests reveal that unionized teachers perform in the bottom percentiles on National Teacher Exams. There are special rooms in the school districts in New York where truly bad teachers are paid outrageous salaries to spend all day playing solitaire because unions prevent administrators from firing them.

"Collective Bargaining is fair," says Bob. Salaries and benefits of over $100,000 for nine months of below average work for a bachelor's degree is above the private sector pay of $40,000 for twelve months of work.

"Collective bargaining gives adjuncts a better deal,...it creates an advantage even Scott Walker might like." I noticed that Lehrman says nothing about what is good and important for students who pay the tuition and have to suffer the socialist indoctrination presented to them on a daily basis. The typical leftist view of egotistical self-interest is coached in doing it for the children. The same children were kept out of school for weeks during the strike in Wisconsin.

Striking in academia should be against the law and it is in some states because it places the self-interest of teachers driven by union membership against the public interest of students' education.

We all watched in dismay as teachers in Wisconsin abandoned their classrooms, dragged their students for weeks on end to protests that they did not understand, taught them that lying is acceptable as long as it is for a good cause, while accepting and presenting bogus sick excuses from bogus doctors.

I have sound advice for adjunct professors who make a career of "adjuncting" in various places in order to have a full time job – perhaps they should move to an area that hires people full-time instead of accepting part-time work and demanding full-time benefits with the help of the SEIU union bosses. We do not need any more unions telling us how to educate our children and what venues their education should take.

Shaping America into Progressivism

Teaching or substituting in America of the early 1980s was not easy. As a Superintendent of Education had told me, they "did not just take anybody off the street. You had to be highly qualified." That did not necessarily mean well versed in a subject matter. You had to belong to the "rarefied" group of licensed teachers.

I was interested in Latin and he had told me that he did not need Latin teachers because he had a person from Latin America who taught Spanish. As I looked at him, I was thinking of the Vice-President who told a crowd in Latin America that, had he paid more attention in his Latin class, he would have been able to speak to his audience in their native language.

The newly formed (1979) Department of Education had instituted stringent rules and regulations that school districts had to follow in order to receive federal funding and state certification. The National Education Association welcomed all dues-paying teachers, eager to indoctrinate them into the master educational plan.

Teaching elementary, middle, and high school required jumping through certification bureaucratic hoops that only the College of Education graduates could easily meet. It was not important if teachers performed well in the classroom, on the National Teacher Exam, or knew their subject area of expertise - they had to be licensed.

Many mediocre students eked out a diploma after four years of easy courses and became distributors of revisionist knowledge and shapers of generations of American students. As they gained tenure, no matter how inadequate their teaching, school districts could not get rid of them. The NEA vehemently defended their rights to a life-long career.

Many former coaches and physical education teachers went back to school for Masters Degrees in School Administration and became principals and superintendents, cheerleaders and supporters of their former colleagues and peers. If they played by the Department of

Education rules, the rewards were plenty. Objective teachers who followed their conscience were marginalized as not being "team players." Non-Education graduates could teach college with a Master's Degree but not in the public schools. Membership in the club had its rewards and prevented better teachers from entering the system.

Liberals took control of education and imposed political correctness, which silenced conservatives and any possible opposition lest they be labeled racists and anti-children.

The curriculum changed from year to year, becoming more secularized and socialist, pushing religion completely out of the public schools. Prayer at football games, singing the national anthem, and the recitation of the pledge of allegiance to our country were scorned. Atheists objected to traditions that made this country great but interfered with their agenda. Being Green, the worship of Gaia, Mother Earth, and activist environmentalism became the new religion.

Teaching methodologies changed yearly, according to the latest fashion from teacher colleges in New York, Boston, California, like a new dress, more outrageous and less conducive to learning but easy on testing and highly experimental. The curriculum became more "socially just." Standards were so relaxed that some students graduated who could not read or write on an elementary level. Education was dumbed down to include even the laziest students, test results worsened, dropouts increased, while knowledge retention declined.

Multilingual education and multiculturalism were forced upon schools in order to accommodate the burgeoning illegal immigrant student population.

A wave of anti-Americanism dominated the lectures of liberals. Everything that America did in its history or stood for became evil and open to negative interpretation. Conservative teachers were silenced by the threat of job loss. Performance boards ignored them but awarded constant praise and "I love myself" certificates to mediocre teachers who played by the progressive rule.

When expressing honest opinions, conservative students were intimidated and ridiculed by socialist activist teachers. Some students received lower grades when their opinions clashed with the teacher's "America is evil" platform. Certain assignments crossed the line of objectivism and had nothing to do with the subject at hand but few parents paid attention or were vigilant enough.

I was shocked when the entire student body was required to attend two-hour indoctrination into the peaceful religion of Islam, presented by a Palestinian imam. A rapt audience of innocent and ignorant high school students was told how respected and cherished Muslim women were. The faculty did not protest but sat stony faced although they all knew the lack of rights and worth of Muslim women. Nobody asked questions about the hangings, stonings, decapitations, and cutting limbs of women under Islam. The religious presentation had been organized by the principal, the same person who said repeatedly that there is a separation of church and state, and refused to allow students to wear crosses to school because it might make students uncomfortable who did not believe in God.

Instead of teaching students that in 235 years of exceptionalism, America rose to become the world's greatest power and revered society, an AP English teacher in Montgomery County, MD was asking students to explain how "Thoreau's extolling the virtues of individualism and self-efficiency can jeopardize the community." They were talking about community in Marxist parlance, as in "communis," Latin for "shared."

We were not allowed to be individuals in the totalitarian regime I lived under for 20 years. We shared a lot of misery, poverty, and despair under communism because self-reliance and rugged individualism were discouraged. Instead, we were told to be sheep under a benevolent government with omnipotent, god-like powers. As Marx said, "A people without a heritage are easily persuaded."

Our children are taught that private property, the lynchpin of liberty, is bad. Thomas Jefferson began the Declaration of Independence with the words, "the pursuit of life, liberty, and property."

Few American students pay attention to what Thomas Jefferson wrote anymore. Distributing condoms to elementary school children and setting up nurseries in high schools across the country for illegitimate babies take precedence over serious education.

American children have been brainwashed to reject the fundamental values of this country and of civilization. The Pew Research Center showed that more Americans age 18 to 29 have a favorable view of socialism over capitalism, 49 percent positive for socialism and 46 percent positive of capitalism. (December 2011)

The United Nation's 150-page "World Happiness Report" promotes European socialism as the path to well-being. Fabian socialism must be imposed on the entire world through social and environmental justice. It is no coincidence that Maryland was the first state in the U.S. to pass The No Child Left Inside Act, forcing environmental literacy as a condition of graduation from high school. The reading and math test scores for some areas in Maryland are pathetic yet students must be environmentally literate in order to protect Mother Earth from the destructive economic activities of man. The education system is clearly pushing the religion of Gaia to the detriment of traditional education.

Article 1, Section 8 of the Constitution lists the items over which Congress has the power to legislate and education is not one of them, neither can education be logically included under the commerce clause. It would be a stretch to consider the Department of Education constitutional. President Carter signed the DOE into law on October 17, 1979 and it began operating on May 16, 1980. President Reagan tried unsuccessfully to dismantle it.

Title 1 of the Elementary and Secondary Education Act of 1965 authorizing $1 billion annually to upgrade schools attended by students of low-income families has grown to $19 in 2010. No Child Left Behind is part of Title 1, an attempt to bring all students to proficiency level in math and reading by 2014. "More than half the states have asked the U.S. Department of Education for a waiver from No Child Left Behind." The Obama's administration will grant the waivers, ten years after President Bush signed the NCLB law, if those states adopt a new set of requirements established by President Obama, Common Core State Standards, a nationalized k-12 program of instruction. Title 1 funding would be tied to the Common Core. The "Race to the Top" grants in 2009 already emphasized "college and career ready" style of teaching and learning. Common Core national standards and tests require states to "surrender control of their classroom" to the federal government. (Heritage Foundation)

The federal government has spent $7 billion a year on Head Start, a program created by President Lyndon Johnson in 1965 to serve almost a million low-income children across the country. Taxpayers have spent $168 billion since its inception yet the National Head Start Impact Study released by the Department of Health and Human Services in January 2010 showed that three and four year olds who were followed into first grade were not impacted positively at all on cognitive skills when compared to those children who did not participate in Head Start.

Congress mandated in 2006 another study of Head Start participants after third grade. Have their cognitive skills perhaps improved then? Health and Human Services concluded the study in 2008 but has not released the study results, four years later. Senators Tom Coburn, Mike Enzi, Lamar Alexander, Richard Burr, and John McCain have asked HHS Secretary Kathleen Sebelius to release the results of the study. (Lindsey Burke)

It is safe to say that the existence of the U.S. Department of Education has had no positive effect on American education in spite of its $70 billion a year budget and its extensive bureaucracy.

Parents disenchanted with public education have proliferated home schooling and charter schools in spite of the vociferous protests of public school teachers, administrators, and NEA.

The worthless Bachelor of Arts has become a piece of paper necessary to get an easy job. Students are disappointed when the six-figure salary job promised by their college advisor does not materialize, after having spent $7,000 per year in a public college on tuition alone.

After taking easy courses and the bare minimum of work, often times hiring other students to write papers for them or do their work, the B.A. degree is not worth the paper it is printed on. Employers request a transcript to verify graduation, but grades and courses taken are rarely scrutinized. Perhaps the students show promise in the perseverance department as potential on-the-job learners.

According to Charles Murray of the American Enterprise Institute, eight million Pell Grants were awarded in 2010, totaling more than $32 billion. New loans of $125 billion were issued by the federal government in the same year.

The sad reality is that college graduates are experiencing 25 percent unemployment in the Obama administration that promised them "hope and change." The hope is gone, there are no jobs in sight, and there is little change left in their pockets when college loans come due.

ECONOMY

2011 - Not the Best Year for America

2011 was not a good year for America, for freedom, for democracy, for law and order. We watched the accelerated disintegration and reshaping of every local, state, and federal institution to the detriment of the American people.

We allowed the leftist minority to push their communist agenda to the point of dismantling traditions dear to generations of Americans who have fought hard to establish the most successful society on the planet.

We watched young people debase themselves publicly. Morality reached a new low of depravity on television, in the streets, on YouTube. Every narcissist and self-indulgent egotistical American looked for fifteen minutes of dubious fame. Our children emulated the depraved Hollywood.

We witnessed the useful idiots, filthy Occupiers of Wall Street, so-called defenders of the ninety-nine percenters, destroy and foul our streets, parks, and monuments with the support of some Democrat Congressmen and the White House. Police looked the other way in the face of millions of dollars worth of property destruction during months of squatting on private or public property. Millions in damages were paid by bankrupt cities and states, by citizens who diligently worked, supported their families, and paid taxes. Occupiers closed down ports in California, interfering with international trade, domestic trade, and the flow of goods while Homeland Security did nothing to prevent the closure.

We watched the main stream media shill for the communist party and communist dictators across the world, while telling American people lies and giving deceptive statistics and falsehoods to support the anti-American agenda of adoring "progressives" in this country.

I never understood why socialists/Marxists called themselves progressives - "regressive" seemed a more appropriate description of their goals. Destroying progress and the capitalist economy is not exactly progressive. Adopting the blue color for socialism-loving Democrats seemed inappropriate since communism by any other name is red, coached in "green" on the outside, fiery red on the inside.

We witnessed the "environmentalist green" proponents weave their "smart-growth" plans to de-develop the United States to the Middle Ages and reduce population growth through crafty health care rationing, outlandish eugenics, and sterilization proposals in order to punish U.S. for the perceived social injustice to third world nations run by tin pot dictators.

We gave developing nations trillions of dollars towards economic development, progress, and to fight poverty, yet we seem to have lost this war since third world nations are just as poor now as they were in the beginning, kept so by the corruption of their leaders and their immediate supervisor, the United Nations.

We saw the end of the expensive war in Iraq that cost us at least $1.5 trillion so far and thousands of dead and maimed on both sides. After eleven years of supposed liberation, nation and democracy building, we are watching the slow takeover of Iraq by Iran, and the certainty of civil war between Sunni and Shia Muslims. Not only were we not reimbursed for the war effort, we did not buy much oil from Iraq; it will be sold to China.

A head of state was deposed while another was assassinated without due process; his pleas for mercy and a fair trial were ignored. The touted Arab Spring turned into an Arab Winter with the Muslim Brotherhood as the victors.

A minority of atheists, agnostics, and Islamists objected to our Christian symbols and traditions dear to all of us - mangers, crosses, and the Bible. Forbidding Christmas displays, Merry Christmas, carols, displaying crosses in public places, and displacing Bibles at Walter Reed Hospital gave fodder to our enemies to push on with the "radical transformation" of America.

Disagreeing with the current regime became hate speech and racism. Following in the footsteps of United Kingdom's intrusive citizen control by a government that knows best no longer seems like a farfetched possibility.

We heard the news media glorify the death of a North Korean tyrant. Reporters and political pundits transformed the murderer of millions into an eccentric saint. The MSM ignored the true hero and patriot, Vaclav Havel, who helped bring the peaceful end to the communist dictatorship. He freed millions of his own people who suffered 45 years of communist oppression. Vaclav had died within days of the butcher Kim Jong Il. Millions shed heartfelt tears for the passing of Vaclav Havel. North Koreans hired professional mourners. North Koreans sighed perhaps in relief but were too frightened, weak, and hungry to show any emotion.

We watched the leftist media stir up the youth in Egypt into Twitter frenzy under the false pretense of democracy and freedom from Mubarak. Every free thinker knew that the Muslim Brotherhood extremists were waiting in the wings to take over the country while oil rich nations were providing money and weapons.

Congress, the Fed, and the White House spent trillions of dollars on schemes, bailouts, and stimuli that benefited foreign governments, domestic and foreign banks, AIG, Goldman Sachs, and created no jobs in America. On the contrary, the jobs czar shipped the GE imaging department overseas. Jobs were not created in our country but in countries like Brazil, Mexico, and Norway with taxpayer money.

The debt-ceiling crisis pointed out the failure of this administration to lead the nation and its success in plunging our economy into insurmountable national debt, a massive threat to our national security.

Corruption had become so rampant, Americans wondered if the famous checks and balances that prevented any one entity from acquiring unbridled power and control over our nation still existed.

Congressional representatives on both sides of the isle legislated against the wishes of the American people, passing law after law in the dead of night, chipping away at our freedoms. Legislators were bribed in order to garner necessary votes.

The Democrat-controlled Senate had not passed a budget in three years, funding government in piecemeal increments with much fanfare and political posturing on the part of the Obama White House and the Democrats. Republicans caved every time, in spite of the fact that voters had given them mandate in the 2010 November elections for lesser government and less spending. As Mark Steyn said, the recent two-month payroll tax cut was "the biggest cave since Tora Bora."

Elections were defrauded by ACORN and voter intimidation remains unpunished to this day. The Justice Department sued state after state that tried to pass laws to protect its borders and financial integrity from illegal immigrants. La Raza organized street protests to demand equal rights with American citizens for "undocumented workers."

Trampling and burning our flag, booing our national anthem, and waving foreign flags at national events and football games became accepted and mundane.

Dropping anchor babies, accepting social welfare, and demanding equal rights with Americans, illegal aliens brought an array of bankruptcies, hospital closings, school closings, unchecked diseases, increased gang violence, gang membership, and drug cartel murders at the border with Mexico. ACLU filed endless lawsuits against defenseless American citizens whose rights and safety were violated.

The leftist "social justice" movement and the "green" movement pushed by United Nations' Agenda 21 and EPA brought us closer and closer to a Marxist dictatorship by a few oligarchs who pulled the strings of our politicians. Lavish union donations kept the campaign coffers of the Democrat party well stocked.

Education became more and more politicized by the left, indoctrinating students into the "global citizen" and the "evil capitalists who are destroying the planet" mentality. Busy and ignorant parents looked the other way, implicitly accepting this indoctrination. More vigilant parents home-schooled their children. Textbooks rewrote history and morality to suit the leftist agenda. The attack on Christianity and Judeo-Christian values intensified.

We experienced more and more censorship on line, in life, in academia, and in print. We became more of a police state, under surveillance for our views, our patriotism, and our military service. TSA received increased powers and authority to strip-search us of our dignity and molest us in the name of public safety.

More and more non-elected bureaucrats gained fiat power over our freedom, our energy, our industry, our speech, freedom of assembly, our health care, choice of schools, banking, finance, land use, water use, and home ownership.

We have high hopes and expectations. 2012 will be the defining moment of our nation – whether we continue to exist as free men and women or cease to exist as a constitutional republic and become another tin pot banana republic dictatorship ruled by a handful of elitist oligarchs.

America is the Sinking Titanic

The Democrat Party is the proverbial iceberg floating on the vast ocean, approaching the mighty Titanic, the most developed, invincible, militarily and technologically able nation on earth, the U.S.A. America has much to fear. Democrat tactics are stealthy, deceptive, well organized, patient, manipulative, and treacherous.

The top of the iceberg looks benign enough, just a group of well-intentioned, caring, almost grandfatherly and grandmotherly individuals who want to protect the downtrodden, the poor, and the middle class from the clutches of the "evil" capitalist corporations, the same corporations who made them rich and put them in power.

The Democrat Party was the party of slavery. It kept the masses in abject poverty, creating a class of perennial victims who could not succeed because were purposefully kept dependent on welfare, handouts, entitlements, and cradle to grave mentality. In exchange for the Democrat largesse, people had to vote Democrat generation after generation.

We live in desperate times – the target of the attack is the American way of life with its large middle class. The National Education Association, the union thugs, the education rent-a-mobs, the harassment, the intimidation, the violent protests organized by SEIU, the offensive speech and hatred towards conservative Americans are precursors of the iceberg threatening to sink the Titanic. The compliant media is watching and ignoring the disaster unfolding, while reporting shamelessly non-stop on the latest scandal in Hollywood.

The administration encourages progressive groups to protest, to get in people's faces, storm their houses and frighten their children. Liberals do not seem to care that our country is broke. We have spent and borrowed into oblivion. "Alea iacta est," (the die is cast), the Democrats want everything and they want it now. Their greedy end always justifies the means.

The Democrats are destroying the well-being of the American families and their ability to earn a living; unemployment and underemployment are at 18%. Discouraged workers lured by 99 weeks of unemployment are at their highest. Steep taxation rates are driving the remaining manufacturing plants overseas and to other states. Tax and spend is the Democrat Party mantra.

Manufacturing used to be the backbone of the middle class because it paid higher wages and stabilized communities. America was a country where you could have a job with a high school degree – these jobs do not exist anymore, they have been shipped elsewhere. Consumers are partly to blame because they stopped buying U.S.-made products as they were more expensive, preferring the cheaper Chinese made goods. It is very hard now to find Made in the U.S.A. goods.

George Soros and his followers have met Bretton-Woods to decide how to re-shape America in his vision and the vision of the One World Government, without any input from the American people.

The Bildebergs have met in Switzerland to decide who will be the next IMF chief and the monetary policy for the rest of the developed world. These people are making policy decisions without any mandate from the American people.

There has been a massive government expansion, TARP, stimulus I and II, cash for clunkers, confiscation of GM and Chrysler with less than a third buyout per share, nationalization of banks, of school loan programs, Fannie Mae, Freddie Mac, health care overhaul, and the destruction of the housing market. "Socially just" programs pushed into law by Democrats forced banks to make loans to people who could not afford to buy a home, had no adequate savings, adequate credit, and no intentions to pay back their loans.

Through lawsuits filed under The Freedom of Information Act, we found out that the Fed had loaned a sizable amount of TARP funds to foreign banks with branches in the U.S. and failed banks such as Indymac and Wachovia.

We saved AIG, the largest insurer, who is also the most Sharia Law compliant corporation in the world. Over half a billion dollars of its profits go to fund jihad all over the world, in accordance with Sharia Law requirements.

TARP beneficiaries never paid back the entire amount given to them and certainly did not pay any interest to the U.S. taxpayers who ultimately are responsible to pay back the huge accumulated national debt.

The stimulus I and II were not meant to give a boost to the economy by financing infrastructure programs, repairing or building roads, bridges, or schools. The stimulus was a money laundering operation to prevent state employees from losing their jobs. By keeping their jobs, these employees paid their union dues, automatically deducted from paychecks, thus enriching the campaign coffers of Democrats. The stimulus I and II were slush funds for political Democrat campaigns and for union-organized protests against ordinary Americans who prefer fiscal responsibility.

Conservatives did not wish to impoverish their children and grandchildren with debt created by irresponsible politicians. Democrats like Reed, Pelosi, and Schumer will be long gone when the bills come due to the next generation of Americans.

Idealist young Americans do not yet understand what awaits them in the future. They are swept up in the communist rhetorical moment of "social justice," forcefully promoted by progressive operatives who are well schooled in Alinsky's "rules for radicals" tactics and by the Democrat Party.

Democrats started an unjust, unprovoked war with Libya that we cannot afford. Nobody is holding Congress accountable for not passing a budget in three years. Republicans and Democrats argued over pitiful reductions in spending of a few billion dollars when we have spent $5 trillion so far. The war with Libya, unauthorized by Congress, must have been a good war because it was a Democrat war. We did not hear a peep from the media that was previously so outraged by Bush's wars. At least he consulted Congress and got their approval instead of going to the United Nations for approval.

How much longer can we borrow from other countries? We are the biggest debtor in the world. The national debt is the biggest threat to our national security. Who are the people who hold our national debt? The Federal Reserve System (the Fed) comes in first place, currently monetizing our debt by printing money, money that is not covered by goods and services, thus eventually leading to inflation.

In second place are other investors in savings and bonds, that is, we the people. Third place is occupied by China. Japan comes in fourth. Mutual fund holdings are fifth. State and local government bonds come in sixth place. Pension funds rank seventh. United Kingdom ranks eighth. Oil exporting nations come in ninth place. Caribbean Banking Center is tenth. AIG, an insurance company that received TARP money is in eleventh place. Brazil, the recent grantee of oil drilling in the Gulf and recipient of $2 billion of U.S. taxpayer money to drill, comes in twelfth. Hong Kong is in thirteenth place. Depository institutions (banks) are in fourteenth place, and last, but not least, Russia.

The year 1971 is remarkable because it is the year in which Nixon ended the backing of U.S. currency by gold and the credit explosion began. "Total U.S. debt increased from $9 trillion in 1971 to $59 trillion today and this excludes unfunded liabilities of anywhere from $70 to $110 trillion." (Egon von Greyerz)

In 2005-2009, the national debt grew from 63.4% to 83.4% of GDP. This debt increase was caused by President Bush's policies. He accomplished this by waging two wars.

After World War II, the national debt briefly reached 100% of GDP. We are driving furiously in that direction under the current administration.

Until the 1980s, the U.S. government had acquired most of its debt either to finance wars or from losses of tax revenues that accompany recessions. After 1980, national debt grew due to government overspending, mild recessions, and financing wars.

Our current options are to either default on the U.S. debt or to monetize it, that is printing $100 trillion to pay the debt off. The Fed has printed $3.3 trillion in two months in 2008 to bail out foreign and domestic banks, propping up institutions that should have been allowed to fail. The bailout weakened our economy and our dollar. That is why gasoline is so high, food is expensive, jobs are scarce, the economy is anemic and bleeding heavily.

Default is a fancy word for bankruptcy – our creditors would ask for payment with our land, mines, property, oil fields, gold, silver, coal, grain, other metals, or indentured servitude.

Monetizing the debt would result in hyperinflation, similar to the Weimar Republic, reducing the value of the dollar to zero, having to carry around wheelbarrows of dollars just to buy a loaf of bread, or burning dollars in the fireplace because it would be cheaper than buying the firewood.

Should nations stop lending us money, we would become persona-non-grata, a sort of third world nation, dragging everybody else with us. People might suffer famine, political unrest, civil disobedience, demonstrations, and wars might ensue in the process. The seemingly innocuous iceberg would definitely sink the Titanic.

Inflation the Economy's Code Blue

In ordinary parlance, when there is a lot of paper or "fiat" (Latin for "let it be") money in circulation, prices go up and our dollars buy less. This is inflation. In two famous photographs of 1923, a German housewife burned "marks" in her kitchen stove because it was cheaper to burn money than to use them to buy firewood and a gentlemen pushed a wheelbarrow full of cash to buy a loaf of bread.

The U.S. government issued its first money in 1862. They were called *greenback*s because of the peculiar green ink that distinguished them from gold certificates. Before greenbacks, banks used paper money called *scrip*. The dollar could be exchanged for fractions of its stated value.

Dollars were backed by gold and silver reserves and, until 1963. U.S. bills were called silver certificates. Today dollars are called Federal Reserve notes and are backed by the economic integrity of the U.S. government. In 1971, the Nixon administration ended the backing of the U.S. dollar by gold and silver.

The oldest surviving paper money is the *Kuan*, issued in China by the Ming dynasty in 1368. Sweden printed the first European bank notes in 1661 and France had paper money in wide circulation in the 18th century. The British issued *promissory notes* in place of paper money. Massachusetts soldiers received these promissory notes in 1690 after the siege of Quebec. There was not much to steal in order to pay the grunts.

The Federal Reserve keeps a count of paper money in circulation by M1, M2, and M3 (money stock). M1 includes all money in spendable or liquid form: cash and money in checking accounts. M2 includes M1, savings, and short-term deposits such as CDs (certificates of deposit). M3 includes M1, M2, and the assets and liabilities of financial institutions such as long-term deposits.

In a strong economy, demand for currency goes up without any

Federal Reserve intervention and the money in circulation goes up. In a weak economy, demand for currency goes down.

When the Fed (Federal Reserve System of banks) follows an *easy money policy* by increasing the money supply, the economy tends to grow, companies hire workers, consumer confidence grows, consumer spending grows, and the economy improves. It would stand to reason that our economy should have rebounded long time ago since the government and the Fed have been spending and printing money as fast as presses, or electronic transfers could go. Unfortunately, money has been going to Europe, the Middle East, and other overseas entities instead of boosting and creating new jobs in the U.S. The rest was squandered on TARP, bailing out GM and Chrysler to the benefit of Fiat and unions, bankrupt green energy companies, unions, Democrat re-election campaign coffers, United Nations, wars, and fomenting "democracy" in the Middle East.

When the Fed adopts a *tight money policy* to slow or combat inflation, the economy worsens, spending typically slows, and unemployment increases. As our economy has worsened, unemployment has climbed, inflation has grown, but the Fed did not adopt a tight monetary policy and government spending has not slowed down, while consumer spending has declined.

We seem to be in an unusual economic period, which defies the traditional economic experience of the past. The intensive care of the U.S. economy has revealed a comatose patient. New factory orders, new housing starts, durable goods, unemployment figures, M2 money supply, the S&P 500 stock index, and the spread between the 10-year Treasury and the federal funds rate are the predictors for our economy's health. If you were an emergency doctor with the finger on the pulse of this American economy under the current administration and Congress, you would be calling code blue.

Consumer confidence and business confidence are also at an all time low, further proof that the U.S. economy, the comatose patient, needs a heart defibrillator. Small business owners are not hiring because they are worried about the liabilities imposed on them by the high record of new regulations passed last year and Obamacare. The looming health care regulations, rationing, uncertainty of fees, penalties for non-compliance, taxes, and costs associated with such a massive bureaucratic undertaking with so many loopholes and exemptions has the potential to bankrupt or destroy many businesses.

The Consumer Price Index (CPI) is the measure of inflation. The

Bureau of Labor Statistics (BLS) calculates CPI each month by recording prices of 80,000 goods and services deemed to reflect the expenditures of a typical urban American consumer: housing, clothing, transportation, health care, recreation, education, and others. Curiously, food and gasoline are not included and Americans know that gasoline prices have more than doubled across the country since President Obama took office. Food prices have also grown steadily.

The CPI uses a baseline year to compare the current inflation rate to, such as 1982-1984. CPI does not take into account the quality of things consumers buy (which affects price) or a consumer's change in taste.

In a recession, the Fed creates money to make borrowing easier and keeps interest rates low. As things pick up, sellers sense rising demand for their products or services and begin to raise prices. The rule of 72 is a guide to assess the impact of inflation. Divide 72 by the reported annual inflation rate to find out how many years it will take for prices to double.

The people hit hardest by inflation are those living on fixed incomes such as retirees. Welfare recipients, Social Security recipients, union contract salaried employees, and government employees receive *COLA* (Cost Of Living Adjustment) remuneration and benefits.

If inflation is slow, it is called *disinflation. Deflation* is a widespread decline in the prices of goods and services. Deflation does not stimulate employment and production because a declining (contractionary) economy puts people out of work and they cannot afford to buy even at cheaper prices.

Runaway inflation, deflation, or defaults on loans, balance-trade-deficits, and bad economic policies are signs of an economy and a country in turmoil. Traders manipulate various currencies by trading on the spot, forward, or swap contracts. Some traders have been banned in certain countries for their illegal and overt attempt to bankrupt their currency.

If you think inflation is a modern phenomenon, consider Diocletian's edict of 301 A.D. to curb inflation. If anyone broke his list of regulations, the punishment was Death. The edict fixed prices for 1,000 items, such as food, raw materials, textiles, transportation, and wages.

When Emperor Valerian was captured by barbarians in 259 A.D., Roman subjects all over the Roman Empire, foreseeing hard times, spent their money on goods, causing 1,000 percent inflation over a period of seventeen years. (Quest for the Past – Reader's Digest editors)

Diocletian's *prices and income* policy did not work but it did not stop him from diverting attention from his government's shortcomings by putting the blame on speculators and rich people. Diocletian's edict preamble blames "men who have nothing better to do than carve up for their own advantage the benefits sent by the gods…men who are themselves swimming in a wealth that would satisfy a whole people, who think only of their gain and their percentage."

I believe that Diocletian's preamble would please the Occupy Wall Street crowd, the unions, people on government dole who pay no taxes, ACORN, the current administration, Hollywood sympathizers of Marxism, and the MSM. They pay constant lip service to "spreading the wealth" and "paying a fair share," without specifying when that "fair share" is enough and why perfectly healthy citizens do not work and prefer to accept government handouts for their entire lives, from someone else's stolen wealth. If I think about it, it is a form of reversed slavery, forcing those who work hard to support those who prefer sloth.

National Debt is a Threat to National Security

National debt is the biggest threat to our national security. Most people's eyes glaze over when discussion turns to business and economics. Americans know we have a huge debt with lots of zeroes but have no idea how it grew so exponentially large, where it came from, who owes it, who owns it, and how many zeroes a trillion has.

Do Americans care who is responsible for this debt, whether we can or should reduce it? Should they just change the channel when the business news flashes across the screen? Few people bother to look at the national debt clock.com, running at nano speed, showing second by second the total indebtedness of each taxpayer, man, woman, and child based on U.S. Congress' policies and current spending of the U.S. government.

The national debt is like a disaster in a faraway place that does not affect or concern us; we can just turn off the news. Even fewer Americans realize that today's economics is the continuation of politics by other means. Our politics and our economy are inexorably intertwined – to understand one, you must examine the other. The Federal Reserve System, our central bank, is never divorced from politics as they pretend. Its Chairman, Ben Bernanke, is a very powerful player as a monetary policy maker.

National debt or public debt is federal government's indebtedness at a moment in time. It is the accumulation of previous budget deficits, the amount by which the government's expenditures exceed its receipts during a specified period of time, usually a year. The government accumulates debt by running deficits because of exorbitant spending. Our government borrows money from U.S. taxpayers via Treasury bills, notes, bonds, foreign investors, and other countries.

We accumulated such huge national debt through wars, recessions, and borrowing to overspend or give away to third world nations. We are borrowing billions we do not have from China in order to fund the Muslim Brotherhood's so called "Arab Spring." This is at a time when our country is broke, several states have suffered devastating tornadoes, floods, fires and FEMA is running out of money. The Middle Eastern budding "democracy seekers," financed and coached by the New World Order proponents, are not so peaceful and friendly to our culture after all and are not really looking for democracy in their countries.

"Since 1971, U.S. borrowed $50 trillion to produce only $13 trillion of goods and services in a 40 year period." Egon von Greyerz, a financial analyst with Matterhorn Asset Management AG in Zurich, Switzerland, said, "From 1971 when President Nixon ended the gold-backing of the dollar, virtually all of the growth in the Western world has come from the massive increase in credit rather than from real growth in the economy." (Craig R. Smith, Crashing the Dollar)

Until the 1980s, the U.S. government had acquired most of its debt either to finance wars or from losses of tax revenues that accompany recessions. Lately, a huge debt was acquired through out-of-control spending and interest payments on borrowing.

After WW II, the national debt briefly reached 100% of Gross Domestic Product, meaning that the monetary value of all goods and services produced in a year equaled total spending. In 2009, the national debt was 83.4% of GDP. President Bush increased the debt by 20% during his presidency and fighting two wars. President Obama exacerbated the problem by adding to the debt burden various giveaways, stimulus I and II, unemployment benefits, the war in Libya, and other financial schemes aimed at deliberately wasting the taxpayer dollars. Economists argue that the current debt, including unfunded liabilities, is anywhere from $110-150 trillion dollars, ten times the predicted amount of the current administration.

Who owns the debt? Domestic citizens, who selfishly wish to have it all right now in order to live well, transfer debt from one generation of Americans to another, to their children and grandchildren. One branch of the U.S. government owes money to another branch and no budget is sacred from dipping into it to take from Peter in order to pay Paul, including Social Security. Their lock box was tampered with long time ago and the key was lost.

The share of the national debt owned by foreign nationals, businesses, and governments is more worrisome as it has been rising rapidly since 2006 when it was over 52% of the total public debt. The top ten holders of American national debt are China, Japan, Caribbean

Banking Center, oil exporters (OPEC), Russia, United Kingdom, Brazil, Luxemburg, Hong Kong, and Taiwan.

It is true, our national debt is measured in dollars, which we can always print in order to meet our payments. This is called monetizing the deficit. Doing so, however, creates inflation, as too much money is chasing too few goods. A responsible government should never print money in outlandish excess of the amount of goods and services produced in a year. If they do, hyperinflation will occur, and severe devaluation of the currency.

The U.S. Consumer Price Index (CPI), also known as inflation, has been stable for 200 years until the early 1900s. From 1971 to 2010, this price index has gone up 500%. Money printing and uncontrolled credit creation are the culprits. Lately, this administration's economists have left out food and gasoline in their measurement of CPI in order to skew reality. This is disingenuous since all Americans are affected by the price of food and gas. According to professors Lawrence H. Officer and Samuel H. Williamson, it took $5.31 to buy in 2008 what it cost $1 in 1971, the year President Nixon ended the backing of the U.S. dollar by gold. Just to keep up with inflation, Americans would have to earn 5.31 times more income today than they did in 1971. Today's dollar is only worth 19 cents when compared to 1971. (Craig R. Smith, Crashing the Dollar)

Uncontrolled national debt can lead to many national security issues: retarded economic growth, lack of capital formation, monetizing deficits (overprinting of money in excess of goods and services thus creating inflation), social turmoil, bankruptcy, revolutions, famine, and war.

The P.I.G.S., Portugal, Italy, Greece, and Spain were reluctantly admitted into the European Union in spite of their high levels of national debt, inflation, and disastrous handling of the economy. Greece, for example, has a 120% ratio of national debt to GDP. We witnessed the turmoil and mayhem in Greece when the government tried to cut the generous social benefits as the only option to curb overspending. None of the European nations who accepted the euro as their national currency could print money to come out of debt, they are dependent on Brussels' EU monetary policy.

Our current policy seems to be putting pressure on the U.S. dollar until two options remain - default on the U.S. debt, or monetizing it by printing more than $100 trillion to pay it.

If we default, as in any case of bankruptcy, creditor nations would demand payment in American assets – our oil fields, mines, land, parks, monuments, buildings, military bases, and even the indentured servitude of generations of taxpayers, similar to the reparations imposed on Germany after World War I. If we default, the dollar would crash.

If we print money ad nauseam, we would trigger a hyperinflation like the Weimar Republic that would also crash the dollar to zero.

We would recover as a society but we would be a former super-power like Greece, Rome, Spain, France, or Britain. Since we are operating in a global trade environment, we would drag the rest of the western world with us as their currencies and economies would crash as well. Famine would ensue in weaker countries and wars in others. (Craig R. Smith – Crashing the Dollar)

The current administration seems to be heading in the direction of national economy and currency obsolescence, forgiving all debts in the process, except global taxes and reparations to America's "victims."

The Super Committee

The Joint Select Committee on Deficit Reduction or as it is known in popular parlance, "The Super Committee," had a deadline to meet. As November 23 approached, 12 Congresspersons failed to make a decision on debt reduction in order to bring under control the lavish spending of the last three years that threatened our national security.

Hillary Clinton, our Secretary of State, said, "I think our rising debt levels pose a national security threat, and it poses a national security threat in two ways: It undermines our capacity to act in our own interest, and it does constrain us where constraint may be desirable. And it also sends a message of weakness internationally." Yet she did not stop giving away our taxpayer dollars to our enemies all over the world.

Admiral Mullen said it more succinctly, "The most significant threat to our national security is our debt."

"The Super Committee is this Constitutional abomination that arose out of the debt ceiling negotiations. It is 12 handpicked representatives of the Senate and House leadership that meet behind closed doors short-circuit everything that is involved in our legislative process, in the parliamentary institutions that have evolved over centuries to distill a common direction from many diverse viewpoints. Their mission is to come up with that decision while side-lining 523 elected representatives of the people of the United States and dump their decisions in the laps of those representatives, for a take it or leave it, up or down vote that cannot even be amended. Bad process makes bad policy and this is the worst process that I have ever seen. Obviously, we will see the repercussions of it when the committee is required to submit its recommendations before Thanksgiving. As you know, the debt limit deal included a so-called sequestration, which initiates automatic spending reductions over a period of ten years if they cannot come to a conclusion. Frankly, I am looking at that as Plan A. (Rep. Tom Mc Clintock, R-Ca)

The twelve members of the "Super Committee" were:
- Rep. Jeb Hensarling (R-Texas), Co-chair

- Sen. Patty Murray (D-Washington), Co-chair
- Sen. Max Baucus (D-Montana)
- Rep. Xavier Becerra (D-Ca)
- Rep. Dave Camp (R-Michigan)
- Rep. Jim Clyburn (D-S.C.)
- Sen. John Kerry (D-Mass.)
- Sen. John Kyl (R-Arizona)
- Sen. Rob Portman (R-Ohio)
- Sen. Pat Toomey (R-Pa)
- Rep. Fred Upton (R-Michigan)
- Rep. Chris Van Hollen (D-Md)

Sequestration was "the cancellation of budgetary resources for the purpose of enforcing statutory budget limits and pay-as-you-go (PAYGO) requirements. This process was triggered automatically when these statutory limits of PAYGO have been violated as a result of legislative actions."

The Balanced Budget and Emergency Deficit Control Act, commonly known as the Gramm-Rudman-Hollings Act, first established the sequestration process in 1985.

The Budget Control Act of 2011 highlighted the following defense budget:

- FY 2011 $530 billion
- FY 2012 President's request $553 billion
- CBO baseline for FY 2013 $549 billion
- President's projection for FY 2013 $571 billion

The automatic trigger returned base line defense budget to FY 2007 levels (adjusted for inflation) and will hold at that level for eight years.

The Budget Control Act of 2011 was divided into two parts:

1. Caps on non-war related discretionary spending for FY 2012 to FY 2021; these caps are further divided into security spending and non-security spending for FY 2012-2013; for FY 2012-2021, a single cap is provided for all discretionary spending (Defense, Homeland Security, Veteran Affairs, National Nuclear Security Administration, the intelligence community, and international affairs)

2. Automatic trigger to force cuts if Congress fails to act on the

recommendations of the Joint Committee or the Joint Committee's recommendations result in less than $1.2 trillion in deficit reduction

The Joint Committee had to approve by a simple majority its deficit reduction plan by November 23, 2011. By December 23, Congress would have held an up or down vote on the Joint Committee bill with a simple majority required for approval. Since a bill with a deficit reduction of at least $1.2 trillion was not approved by both chambers nor signed into law by the President by January 15, 2012, the trigger provision automatically took effect and the defense budget became $472 billion.

According to the Center for Strategic and Budgetary Assessments, the patterns of the 112th Congress has been of "management by crisis," beginning with the near government shutdown in April 2011 and the narrowly avoided government default on August 2, 2011. (Todd Harrison)

According to the Washington Post headline, "Tax Issue Handcuffs Super Committee." The twelve lawmakers did not agree on a basic framework.

- Republicans refused to raise taxes
- Republicans rejected the President's deal to cut federal health and retirement programs in exchange for $1 trillion in new revenue over the next decade
- Automatic reductions would have fallen heavily on the Pentagon
- Democrats refused to commit to specific entitlement cuts
- Republicans suggested that tax collections should rise solely through economic growth
- Super Committee suggested to cut entitlement spending and to close several tax loopholes
- Super Committee suggested that tax-writing committees overhaul the tax code to lower rates and raise sufficient additional revenue to meet the $1.2 trillion target
- Others urged the Super Committee to count the savings of approximately $1.1 trillion over the next decade from the drawdown in Iraq and Afghanistan towards the $1.2 trillion reduction in the deficit reduction bill; House Majority Leader Eric Cantor (R-Va) criticized such war savings as "gimmicks

and accounting tricks."

Sen. John McCain (R-Ariz.), in his infinite wisdom, promised to defuse the trigger through legislation if the Super Committee did not come to an agreement.

Unlike S&P, which downgraded our country's credit worthiness status, Moody has decided to uphold the AAA rating in August because "more than $2 trillion in deficit reduction was at least planned."

The Department of Defense was advised to make contingency plans for sharp cuts as required by the trigger in FY 2013.

The Romans had a very wise motto, "Si vis pacem, para bellum," "If you want peace, prepare for war." As we lower our ability to defend ourselves against enemy threats, consider what uncontrolled national debt has lead to in other countries:

- Bankruptcy
- Lack of capital formation
- Retarded economic growth
- Monetizing deficits (overprinting of money in excess of goods and services produced in the economy thus causing inflation; the Federal Reserve System Chairman Bernanke calls this overprinting of money euphemistically "quantitative easing," or QE)
- Social turmoil, famine, revolutions

Not paying our national debt is not an option. When Venezuelan dictator Cipriano Castro who borrowed lots of money in early 20th century and refused to pay it back when payment was demanded, in December 1902 warships from Italy, Britain, and Germany shelled Venezuelan forts and blockaded the country's ports until Caracas paid up.

If our government borrows more money, more pressure would force us to cut defense spending and it would be painfully evident proof that we are becoming a comatose superpower.

Mortgage Meltdown

In early 2008, my husband and I were looking to purchase a house. We were very careful, looking for a home that we needed and could afford, not a home that we wanted. As we visited various builders, we began to notice mortgage brokers busy with clients in various processes of finalizing contracts. The buyers were of modest income, some did not speak English at all, but purchasing half a million dollar plus homes in upscale neighborhoods. I was surprised that so many lower income people would qualify for such an astronomical purchase, the most expensive item the average American buys in his/her lifetime.

There were thousands of houses for sale, mostly short sales, bank owned, with droves of bidders competing to buy them as home prices were still climbing. We quickly realized how difficult it would be to purchase a finished house. For every bid we made, thirty prospective buyers would out bid us. One man owned seven homes and was still buying more since flipping was very profitable. I fell in love with one house but nobody knew who owned it, the deed had been passed around quickly so many times, the realtor had no idea where it was.

We finally made a decent offer on a home owned by Indymac of California. We waited a couple of months and, as we received no answer, decided to build our own. Six months later, after we had broken ground for our new home, Indymac called us to proceed right away with the purchase, preferably in one day. They were trying to sell as much of their toxic mortgage loans as possible.

Indymac had just been closed down by the Fed. A congressional representative from New York caused a run-on-the bank after discussing its insolvency publicly. Indymac was the first victim of the mortgage meltdown of toxic assets that was to follow: Lehman Brothers, Countrywide, etc.

As a person who worked hard my entire life to purchase a home and pay it off, I was personally victimized by the mortgage meltdown since the house I still own is rotting away unsold. I played by the rules, the rules of honest, responsible, and hard-working Americans, who paid their mortgages, their taxes, gave to charity, and followed the law.

Jimmy Carter and Bill Clinton pushed the Community Reinvestment Act of 1977. Spreading the wealth seemed like a great socialist idea – take from producers and give to people who made no effort to better themselves, study and work. They were more than happy to take from the government, having no idea nor caring who was actually paying for their welfare.

Feelings of pride for a job well done and putting in a good day's work were lost during forty years of welfare and entitlements designed to create perennial Democrat voters enslaved to the federal government. Cradle to grave entitlements mentality created people who lost their purpose, pride, and responsibility to themselves and their families. There was no surprise when welfare-dependent people waited on local and federal governments to save them from the on-coming hurricane Katrina.

President George Bush made many attempts to rein in the mortgage abuse. A Democrat-controlled Congress overrode seventeen attempts made at accountability. Lawmakers like Maxine Waters, Barney Frank, and Chris Dodd, all Democrats, maintained that giving 100 percent mortgages to people who had shady credit and insufficient income worked well and protected the poor. They claimed that home ownership was a right and denying it was discriminatory and racist.

The happy beneficiaries of the Ponzi scheme mortgage loans called Community Reinvestment Act, which was bound to crash at some point, participated willingly in the destruction of other people's lives and wealth. Why would they care if other Americans saved their money, were responsible citizens, bought homes they could afford, made payments on time, paid all their bills, and maintained a good credit rating? Although on welfare, it was their right to own a home, said ACORN through bullhorns, while picketing bankers' homes.

Laurie, a former mortgage broker and advertising executive, called a national syndicated talk show host and described how the mortgage-backed securities were pushed by Congress at the height of the real estate price rise in 1999-2003. Fannie Mae, Freddie Mac, HUD, and FHA had representatives who visited mortgage/brokerage offices quite often, putting pressure on agents to get as many mortgages out of the door as possible.

Laurie continued, mortgage companies would get $15 million worth of " wholesale line of credit" with the guarantee that Fannie and

Freddie would buy them immediately, repackage them, or send them whole to Lehman Brothers. Mortgage brokers doubled and tripled during this period because of the wholesale lines of credit. Banks that were heavy into wholesale lines of credit went under like WAMU, Countrywide, Indydmac, etc.

According to this caller, few knew in the beginning that 95 percent of these loans were insolvent, in the sub-prime category, although they were not rated that way. The executives at Freddie and Fannie would pay themselves huge bonuses for a job well done.

"According to the people from the Credit Managers Bureau, the three major credit rating agencies were under pressure from the government, Congress, FHA, Fannie, Freddie, to fix customers' credits in order to qualify them for the loans. A "rapid re-score process" was developed that allowed mortgage offices to write a sentence explaining someone's bad credit issues and score of 580 and, within an hour of faxing it to the credit bureau, a good credit score of upwards of 700 appeared." (Laurie on the Rush Limbaugh Show)

"For the non-income call mortgages, people who were self-employed, did not have a W-2 or 1099 form, or did not have income at all to show that they qualified for a loan, the rapid re-score process was used. The rapid re-score was employed only for mortgage purposes although brokers friends used rapid re-score to buy cars. When the next credit update from the major credit bureau agencies took place, the good credit rating of 700 plus disappeared and the old low credit score was reinstated." (Laurie on the Rush Limbaugh Show)

Laurie continued that the vast majority of non-income qualifying loans were 2-3 year adjusted rate mortgages (ARMs), written during 2003-2005. By the end of 2006, the two-year ARMs had begun to circulate, had become due, and people had to refinance their house. They now had to pay a reasonable interest rate (not just 2.5 percent) plus a regular amortization schedule. Owners had to pay principal down every month and payments were 4-5 times higher than the original payment. A mortgage of $1,000 per month now rose to $4,000-5,000 per month.

Unscrupulous companies on the east coast started to buy bundled mortgages of businesses that had already started to go bad. They even bought some from Lehman Brothers. As real estate prices were still going up, the investor groups negotiated people out of their homes, gave them back what they could, sold the mortgages to qualified buyers and, for a short time, the scheme was successful. At the same time, those who were negotiated out of their homes complained that they did not get enough money. At the end of the day, people who played by the rules were hurt. Four different states are prosecuting these unscrupulous companies under Racketeer Influenced and Corrupt Organizations Act (RICO).

Investors stepped in to buy the mortgages with late payments since home prices were still climbing. At this point, there was a lot of poison ingested into the housing market and nobody knew exactly the extent of the poison.

"Fannie and Freddie spread this stuff out so far and so wide, you would have had to have been on the ground floor to realize how much, millions, billions, trillions of these securities were floating around on the open market. Rapid re-scores were in one package and non-income mortgages were in another package." (Laurie on the Rush Limbaugh Show)

According to the caller, Fannie and Freddie were pushing these mortgages so extensively that they had booths at all the mortgage seminars, like "carnival booths." "They were so excited that you were in the mortgage business. You could rapidly re-score 500,000 people a year and they would back up and buy anything you could send them."

"The government and wealthy people gave us the mortgage meltdown. They knew it was coming in 2008 in the middle of a presidential campaign. They gave us the financial panic in 2008, TARP, and Paulson, the former CEO of Goldman Sachs as Treasury Secretary. They knew George Bush would be blamed for everything." Bush made the wrong choice of Treasury Secretary and exacerbated the problem. Lehman Brothers were not bailed out because they were not Goldman Sachs.(Laurie, Rush Limbaugh Show)

As I ponder the mortgage meltdown, I come to the realization that the people who caused the loss of trillions of dollars of wealth to the American people are still in power, lecturing us on how irresponsible we are in our lives, our spending habits, our energy use, fuel use, and general uncontrollable quest for consumption while we hurt the planet.

Obama's Inflation

I enjoy shopping at my neighborhood grocery store. The shelves are always well stocked, there is a wide variety of food to satisfy even the most finicky palates, and prices are reasonable. Unfortunately, prices have steadily risen with each trip in response to the current administration's expanding fiscal and monetary policies. My well-grounded fear is that shelves will be empty in the near future.

Prices of corn, wheat, and rice have risen sharply on the Chicago Board of Trade due to severe flooding and other natural disasters. Using corn unwisely as a bio-fuel further exacerbated the shortage of corn. Some countries experienced diminished corn and wheat crops due to severe water shortage.

Monetizing the budget deficit by the Federal Reserve System (the Fed), printing money non-stop without backing of goods and services, has the unpleasant side effect of ballooning prices, also known as inflation. In plain English, too much money is chasing too few goods, resulting in higher prices for commodities and services.

Because most goods, including food, are trucked or shipped via trains and airplanes from great distances, and are produced and harvested with equipment that requires Diesel or gas, the higher cost of fuel must be factored into the rising cost.

You could say, like the Democrats, that the Republicans are at fault because President Bush started two wars in the Middle East thus disrupting supply. You could also add the war in Libya started by President Obama. However, so many variables beside supply affect the price of oil and thus the price of everyday goods and services.

President Obama just gave new leases to British Petroleum and Petrobras of Brazil to drill in the Gulf of Mexico while imposing a moratorium of seven years on domestic drilling. You could say that there is a purposeful domestic disruption of supply by the Obama administration.

You could also say that it was President Obama's plan from the beginning to drive up oil prices to European levels since he made a well-documented statement that under his administration gas prices will "necessarily skyrocket." I am not sure what his intentions are, perhaps he is trying to save the planet from unnecessary pollution; I would like to believe that he is not trying to impoverish the nation on purpose. Europeans have been paying $4-8 per gallon of gas for years, depending on the country, and depending on how socialist the ruling government is.

You could also blame the high gas prices on greedy oil companies who increase their prices just to "take advantage of the little people." Obama uses such platitudes but hides the fact that the margin of profit for oil companies is much lower than Apple's, yet nobody complains about the greedy profiteers that make our electronic gadgets and iPhones. Liberals hypocritically complain about pollution and big oil although some of them own shares in oil companies or have fortunes tied to the oil industry.

You could blame speculators on the Chicago Board of Trade for high crude prices as Democrats have done during the Bush administration. Price per barrel of oil reached $140 when gas was over $3 per gallon. Liberals were outraged when gas exceeded $3 a gallon, trashing Republicans. Under President Obama, oil is $100 per barrel of crude oil and $4 per gallon of gasoline, yet liberals are silent, even making excuses why $4 a gallon is a positive development. Only a moronic progressive could spin the disastrous price of the commodity that drives the energy of our economy into a feel-good psychobabble excuse.

President Obama is strangely detached from the expanded misery and class warfare that his policies have created for most Americans. Talking in continuous campaign mode and eerily detached, he criticizes the very policies he has put in place that have failed.

He is condescendingly advising Americans to trade in gas guzzling SUVs for GM electric cars. Homes may catch fire while recharging simultaneously thousands of cars, blackouts may occur from power overload, but that is thinking too far ahead.

How is he going to generate all electricity needed if he intends to bankrupt the coal industry and we do not have enough nuclear power or hydroelectric plants? How is wind and solar power going to generate enough energy to run the world's largest economy?

The President is recommending that people get used to hard times. He told an adoring crowd of young people in Palo Alto, Ca during a Facebook town hall meeting that they should get used to a lower standard of living because the Republican proposal to cut spending will be so drastic, Social Security and welfare, including Food Stamps, will be destroyed. None of this is true; Paul Ryan's proposal aimed to save Social Security and Medicare. President Obama conveniently forgot to mention that his second Stimulus cut Medicare to seniors in half and Food Stamp programs in order to finance teacher union salaries and pensions in several blue states and funded Michelle Obama's pet program, healthy school lunches.

He launched into describing how his mother had to be on Food Stamps for a short period while studying for her Ph.D. We are not sure food stamps were available at that time since the program started in its current form in 1977. There is no evidence that his statement is true and he has never mentioned this story before in any of his books.

The indefinite and never-ending War on Poverty launched by President Johnson's Great Society is today the fastest growing component of government spending. Forty million Americans received food stamps in 2010 and the U.S. Department of Agriculture projected it to be 43 million in 2011. As Wyoming U.S. Senator Alan Simpson, a member of Obama's National Commission on Fiscal Responsibility and Reform, so aptly said, the Federal Government's biggest social program is "a milk cow with 310 million t*ts." In 2009, the Heritage Foundation determined that so far, $17.6 trillion in welfare have been dispersed to the so-called poor. America appears to have lost the War on Poverty.

Nobody is addressing the real culprit of high gas prices, the destruction of the U.S. dollar, the currency in which gasoline is priced. The U.S. dollar is the Free World's "reserve currency" as established by the Bretton Woods conference. Oil is purchased internationally using the U.S. dollar as the global medium of exchange.

There is an inverse relationship between the value of the U.S. dollar and the price of oil, the weaker the dollar, the higher the price of oil. A weak dollar also results in people wanting to hold more precious metals such as gold, silver, and platinum, resulting in higher prices of these commodities.

The first in line affected by the current inflation and high energy prices are the elderly because they live on fixed incomes. Since pensions may or may not be adjusted for inflation, the problem is compounded. Some pensions and Social Security give a Cost of Living Adjustment (COLA). That is a very small number when compared to the doubling of prices on some goods and services that the elderly use on a daily basis.

Social Security checks were not adjusted for inflation last year and are not going to be adjusted this year either. I take issue with Social

Security being considered an entitlement since many beneficiaries have actually paid for decades into the non-existent Social Security Trust Fund.

The Obama administration does not seem concerned with addressing the dire issue of inflation caused by its overspending and out of control money printing. Furthermore, gas and food should be included in the CPI index when calculating the true value of current inflation.

The dollar value can go to zero, as the Germans learned in 1920s with their currency under the left-liberal Weimar Republic. Jens O. Parssons explains in the book, "Dying of Money: Lessons of the Great German and American Inflations," how the debasing of currency destroys people and nations.

Redistribution of Wealth, The Democrat Party's Socialist Plan

The Communist Party confiscated my grandparents' and my parents' land, homes, guns, jewelry, gold coins, paintings, wedding pictures, clocks, watches, bonds, stocks, tools, savings, and anything of value. They left my grandparents homeless. Grandpa and Grandma had to build a barn-like structure made of mud and straw bricks, which they called home. My Grandparents refused to relocate from the rural area into grey concrete apartment cubicles in the city. My parents chose the one bedroom apartment with its low rent, subsidized by the government.

I am staring at my 50-year-old house, empty, sad, and abandoned. We spent 18 wonderful years within its walls. The formerly lush surroundings are now overgrown with weeds and kudzu. We trimmed the azalea bushes; they are making a comeback with beautiful pink, purple, and fuchsia blooms. The rose bushes are sprouting a few anemic, tiny flowers.

I know where Tiger's tomb is by the overgrown cluster of daffodils. The only hardy survivor is the fig tree, planted when the house was built. It has grown taller since I last saw it. It is covered with blooms – birds and squirrels will be happy when the sweet fruits ripen later in the summer. The Japanese magnolia, or what is left of it after Katrina, is a symphony of pink beauty. In a few days, it will snow petals in a thick carpet all over the yard.

The house has been empty for over two years now, a victim of the mortgage market crash, crash brought on by the Democrats forcing banks to lend money to citizens who could not possibly afford a home or pay it back. The area is so economically depressed. Renting and selling are equally impossible. There are two other empty homes on a small street of ten houses. It is an ideal place, quiet, lovely, and close to everything.

The Democrats enlisted the help of nefarious organizations such as SEIU, ACORN, community agitators, and other street organizers to picket the homes of bankers to force them to lend money to non-credit worthy customers under the false charge of racism. Once the loans were approved, with very little checking of documentation, the bankers had no choice but to package bad mortgage loans with good ones and resell them to others in order to minimize loss. Bankers are in business to make money for their stockholders, not redistribute wealth among citizens.

Realtors received their cut of the bad mortgage deals. They helped people they knew could not afford such lavish and expensive homes on their incomes. Paperwork was misfiled, salaries stretched, proof of income and bad credit scores overlooked or emergency rescored for a fee.

Banks sold and resold bad mortgages so quickly and so many times that current owners had no idea which bank held their mortgage contracts. Trying to purchase such a home was impossible, nobody knew who owned it.

Some citizens took advantage of the housing boom by flipping homes quickly in order to make huge profits. They are guilty parties to the housing disaster. Financially irresponsible people who bought homes on interest-only schemes knew they were taking a huge risk.

Jimmy Carter and Bill Clinton pushed the Community Reinvestment Act of 1977. Spreading the wealth seemed like a great socialist idea – take from producers and give to people who made no effort to better themselves, study and work , happy to take from the government, having no idea or caring who was actually paying for their welfare.

Feelings of pride for a job well done and putting in a good day's work were lost during forty years of welfare and entitlements designed to create perennial Democrat voters enslaved to the federal government. Cradle to grave entitlements mentality created people who lost their purpose, pride, and responsibility to themselves and their families. There was no surprise when welfare dependent people waited on local and federal governments to save them from the on-coming hurricane Katrina.

Bush the son made a weak attempt to stop the mortgage abuse but it was not enough. A Democrat-controlled Congress overrode several attempts made at accountability. Corrupt lawmakers like Maxine Waters, Barney Frank, and Chris Dodd, all Democrats, maintained that giving 100% mortgages to people who had shady credit and insufficient income worked well and protected the poor. They maintained that home ownership was a right and denying it was discriminatory and racist.

These happy beneficiaries of the Ponzi scheme mortgage loans called Community Reinvestment Act, which was bound to crash at some point, participated willingly in the destruction of other people's lives and wealth. Why would they care if other Americans saved their money, were responsible citizens, bought homes they could afford, made payments on time, paid all their bills, and maintained a good credit rating? Although on welfare, it was their right to own a home, said ACORN through bullhorns, while picketing bankers' homes.

I studied years and years in college when people my age were having fun, partying every weekend, enjoying their youth, reproducing irresponsibly, dropping out of school, drinking, doing drugs, smoking, abusing their bodies in general, and expecting society to pay for their wasted years because it is "social justice." Am I supposed to spread my wealth now to the leeches of society who chose the path of sloth and convenience?

I pay enough in taxes to support other people's children, irresponsible lifestyles, illegal aliens' free education, housing, and healthcare. I am also generously donating to causes that help people during natural disasters or stricken by unfortunate circumstances.

I would like to see rich liberals, Hollywood, and politicians in Washington put their money where their lecturing mouths are and spread their wealth first, give away personal fortunes before they take our hard-earned property and savings.

I worked 18 years to pay off my house. I went to work when I felt bad, when I felt tired, ill, or overworked, very seldom calling in sick. I held two jobs most of the time in order to take care of my family. I did not take vacations, bought expensive gadgets we did not need, and did not update the house with the latest appliances, furniture, or interior decor. It was clean, warm, cozy and homey. I kept it well repaired, but it was dated. It was our home, solidly built, with a tornado shelter and six-foot walls. Homes this sturdy are no longer built lest you spend a fortune. We had well insulated walls, double windows and doors before the environmental nut jobs were even born. Now, it is sitting empty and decaying, a sign of the economic and financial troubles that are destroying our country, all caused by greed, irresponsibility, politicians in general, and the Democrat Party in particular. Eighteen years of diligent and responsible work are dripping slowly down the economic drain, all in the socialist name of "spreading the wealth."

Spending America into Oblivion

The United States Government Accountability Office (GAO) released the Report to the Secretary of the Treasury involving the financial audit of the Bureau of Public Debt's (BPD) "Fiscal Years 2011 and 2010 Schedules of Federal Debt."

Every page is definitive proof that our country is truly broke. Our national debt is so large that measures must be taken immediately to address the out of control spending that is going to burden future generations yet unborn and destroy our economic superpower status.

Since 1997, GAO audits the Bureau of Public Debt annually to determine if schedules are reliable and BPD maintains effective control over financial reporting "relevant to the Schedule of Federal Debt." GAO "tests compliance with selected provisions of laws related to the Schedule of Federal Debt."

The Department of the Treasury manages the federal debt. Our federal debt is composed of Treasury securities held by the public and federal government accounts called "intra-governmental debt holdings." These holdings represent 230 federal agencies, one agency owing money to another.

Debt held by the public represents the amount of money the federal government has borrowed from the public to finance "cumulative cash deficits." Cumulative cash deficits represent all the previous years' deficits combined.

The public is comprised of individuals, corporations, state or local governments, the Federal Reserve System (our so-called central bank), and foreign governments. The majority of debt is in the form of Treasury securities such as bills, notes, bonds, and Treasury Inflation-Protected Securities (TIPS) that are sold through auctions and then resold by whoever owns them.

"Intra-governmental debt holdings represent federal debt owed by Treasury to federal government accounts – primarily federal trust funds such as Social Security and Medicare – that typically have an obligation to invest their excess annual receipts (including interest earnings) over disbursements in federal securities."

Americans who pay taxes and pay attention (pun intended), know that there are no such trust funds or "lock boxes" for Social Security and Medicare. The money is spent when receipts come in from taxpayers.

"Most federal government accounts invest in 'special nonmarketable Treasury securities' that represent legal obligations of the Treasury and are guaranteed for principal and interest by the full faith and credit of the U.S. government."

Debt holdings between government's agencies are not shown as balances on the government's consolidated financial statements because they represent one agency of the federal government owing another under "U.S. generally accepted accounting principles." "When the federal government's financial statements are consolidated, those offsetting balances are eliminated."

Debt held by one agency to another does not typically require cash payments from the current budget (they are electronic voodoo credits) and are thus not considered a burden on the current economy. Intra-governmental debt and interest payments are a claim on future resources and a burden on future taxpayers and the future economy that must make good on the electronic credits. "When federal trust funds redeem Treasury securities to obtain cash to fund expenditures, Treasury usually borrows from the public to finance these redemptions."

Debt held by the public is considered more real and a burden on today's economy because it is cash. Borrowing from the public absorbs resources that should be available for private investment. It thus crowds out private investment. Interest paid on this debt reduces budget flexibility since it cannot be controlled directly.

GAO found out during its audit that during the last 4 fiscal years, total federal debt has increased by $5.788 trillion or 64 percent, from $8.993 trillion as of September 30, 2007 to $14.781 trillion as of September 30, 2011.

"The increases to total federal debt over the past 4 fiscal years represent the largest dollar increases over a 4-year period in history."

Rounding the numbers and presenting them in trillion dollars, our federal debt has increased from $8.9 trillion in 2007 to $14.8 trillion as of September 30, 2011.

The Treasury declared a debt issuance suspension period from May 16, 2011 through August 2, 2011. "Treasury utilized a number of extraordinary actions within its legal authorities to avoid exceeding the debt limit."

The extraordinary actions undertaken by the Treasury included suspending investments to:

- Government Securities Investment Fund of the Federal Employees' Retirement System
- Civil Service Retirement and Disability Fund (CSRDF) and disinvesting a security held by CSRDF
- the Postal Service Retiree Health Benefits Fund (Postal Benefits Fund)
- Exchange Stabilization Fund (ESF)
- New issuances of state and local government securities from May 6-August 1, 2011

On August 2, 2011, the Budget Control Act of 2011 was enacted by Congress and signed into law, which increased the statutory debt limit by $400 billion on August 2, 2011, and by $500 billion on September 22, 2011.

The U.S. Government Accountability Office reports, "The debt held by the public has increased from roughly 62 percent of Gross Domestic Product (GDP) at the end of fiscal year 2010 to roughly 68 percent at the end of fiscal year 2011."

GDP represents the monetary value of all final goods and services produced in a year in the U.S. Six percent of our GDP has been squandered in one year by this administration on various schemes, bailouts, stimuli, and faux job creations.

Treasury reporting shows that foreign ownership of Treasury securities represents a significant portion of debt held by the public, 46 percent as of June 30, 2011. In the last ten years, June 30, 2001-June 30, 2011, Treasury International Capital estimates securities held by foreign and international investors to be $4.51 trillion. In ten years, the debt to foreigners rose from $983 billion in 2001 to $4.501 trillion.

Overview of federal debt managed by the Bureau of Public Debt:

- Gross Federal Debt Outstanding in 2011 is $14.781 trillion
- Interest expense in 2011 is $454 billion
- Fifty-nine percent or $5.625 trillion debt will mature within the next 4 years
- Intragovernmental debt holdings of 230 individual federal agencies consist primarily of balances in the Social Security, Medicare, Military Retirement and Health Care, and Civil Service

Retirement and Disability trust funds, 91 percent of the $4.654 trillion

- Interest paid on Treasury marketable securities is 0.1% for T-bills, 2.3% for T-notes, 5.8% for T-bonds, and 2.8% for nonmarketable Treasury securities
- Federal Debt held by the public includes debt held by the Federal Reserve Bank (FRB) of New York in the System Open Market Account (SOMA) holdings for the purpose of conducting monetary policy

SOMA (System Open Market Account), managed by the Federal Reserve Bank of New York, contains dollar-denominated assets acquired via open market operations and is used as collateral for U.S. currency in circulation.

The Government Accountability Office demonstrates with current numbers how truly broke our country is and the "unsustainable fiscal path driven by structural imbalance between revenues and spending for major entitlement programs." In order to prop up the fragile economy, the Government Accountability Office (GAO) recommends that immediate action must be taken involving both federal spending and revenue. (Source GAO)

Debut of Made-In-China Social Security Checks

The total federal budget for 2012 is $3.68 trillion. The interest on debt is $242 billion. The rest constitutes mandatory and discretionary spending.

Discretionary spending refers to the budget APPROPRIATED each year. The discretionary budget is one third of the federal budget. Congress directly sets the level of discretionary spending ($1.24 trillion) and can choose to increase or decrease any programs.

In 2012, 57 percent of the federal discretionary budget is national defense. The rest includes education, health programs, and housing assistance.

Mandatory spending ($2.44 trillion) includes entitlement programs, funded by eligibility rules or payment rules. Congress decides to create a program, determines who is eligible for the program, various criteria, and then estimates how much is appropriated for the program each year based on how many people will be eligible and will apply for benefits.

Social Security, Medicare, and Medicaid are the most costly entitlement programs. Veterans Administration programs, federal employee and military retirement plans, unemployment compensation, food stamps, and agricultural price supports are also included in entitlement programs.

Congress periodically reviews the eligibility rules and may change them in order to exclude or include more people.

Mandatory spending makes up about two-thirds of the total federal budget. The largest mandatory program is Social Security, about one-third of mandatory spending. As the age demographic of the country shifts towards an older population, mandatory spending increases.

The controversial national debt or public debt is $14 trillion to $100 trillion, depending on how many variables are considered. Nobody disputes the fact that, over the years, U.S. ran more deficits than surpluses because of recessions, inflation, sluggish growth, wars, oil price shocks, and a steady growth in entitlements.

Two American presidents are largely responsible for entitlements, Franklin D. Roosevelt and Lyndon B. Johnson with the "New Deal" and the "Great Society." All politicians recognized the popularity of the programs and considered it political suicide to reduce or repeal the benefits once extended. Tip O'Neill called entitlements the "third rail of politics."

Promising costly benefits to individuals predicated on an unsustainable Ponzi scheme eventually caught up with countries like Portugal, Italy, Greece, and Spain, especially since their governments gave up their sovereignty and could no longer control respective monetary policies, they were at the mercy of the European Union and its currency, the euro. It is heading in that direction for the United States. Right now, our temporary salvation is the fact that we can print dollars.

Several administrations changed tax policies, thus altering revenue; new unregulated financial instruments were invented and sold as debt securities to financial markets, creating the capability to finance large debt, and the capability to create dangerous bubbles that could burst.

To service a debt, sufficient cash on hand must repay interest and some principal over time. Normal operating expenses of our country should be fully funded with current tax revenues in order to preserve borrowing capacity for future crises.

If the president tells Social Security recipients that they may not get their checks if the debt ceiling is not raised, he is in essence telling them that he does not have any Social Security lock box money, it has been spent long time ago and he must borrow from the Chinese in order to make payments on the Social Security Ponzi scheme. This should give Americans great pause.

For the past three decades, the government has used deficit spending (spending more money than it receives in taxes) in order to cover operating expenses, stealing from Peter to pay Paul. Some economists argue that deficit spending is necessary during recessionary periods. We can all agree that it cannot be sustained indefinitely if it exceeds the growth rate of the economy.

How does the government raise money in order to finance the debt? The Department of the Treasury's Bureau of Public Debt attracts buyers and arranges for the sale of debt instruments: Treasury bills, notes, bonds, and inflation protected securities. Bills mature in less than a year, notes in two to ten years, and bonds mature in twenty to thirty years. Inflation protected securities (TIPS) are sold in various maturities and are indexed to the rate of inflation. Said securities are sold directly or on secondary markets.

As the U.S. runs more and more debt, the Treasury must find new sources of financing or enforce stricter revenue collection (taxes). Sealed bid auctions are held to finance new debt and to roll over existing debt that has matured and is still outstanding.

About 36 percent of public debt will come due within a year ($1.6 trillion) and another $3.5 trillion over the next three years. In 2009, the Treasury held an auction on average more than once a day to finance $7 trillion of new and maturing debt.

How much more debt will international and domestic investors absorb before reaching a tipping point since the Federal Reserve has kept interest rates so low over an extended period? The more debt U.S. amasses, the more pressure will be put on the Fed to raise interest rates.

Central banks hold reserves in U.S. dollars as a hedge against their own currencies. The price of oil is quoted in U.S. dollars. There is pressure to change that as the economic and political strength of the United States wanes.

The sheer scale of borrowing necessary to sustain growing U.S. deficits, the possibility of default, and the bleak outlook of U.S. economic prosperity because of the recent housing collapse "could well exceed the absorption capacity of Asian central banks for dollar holdings."

International trade deficits could contribute to the devaluation of the dollar, driving interest rates upward in order to attract more foreign and domestic investment that would sustain our insatiable spending appetite.

As long as investor confidence in the U.S. government exists, there is no danger that investors will dump the dollar in favor of some other currency or gold, triggering a stampede sell-off in U.S. stocks and bonds. Rising interest rates alone could plunge the world into a global financial crisis.

Voracious government demand for credit can "crowd out" private sector investment, causing high unemployment and lack of capital formation. Creditors can choose to lend their money to the government instead of buying corporate stocks and bonds.

If business confidence is low because small business owners see higher taxes in the future or are uncertain about future government regulations, private investment will be "crowded out" resulting in more unemployment or lack of new job creation. Industrial base will weaken, the competition will diminish, research and development will dwindle, and acquisition costs will go up.

"America is like no other dominant power in modern history – because it depends on other countries to sustain its military and economic dominance." A strong economy supports a strong military, and a strong military supports statecraft.

Past decisions on debt increasingly limit the ability of the government to maneuver economically and to deal with national emergencies such as war by running large deficits. The government runs large deficits now just to maintain the status quo. This "leaves the country more exposed to shocks and more vulnerable to the financial leverage of its creditors."

Thomas Jefferson summed up the quandary best when he said, "The laws of nature made it unfair to impose the debts of one generation upon another." Perhaps, instead of nation building in Iraq, Afghanistan, Libya, and other countries that do not understand nor want democracy, who are not grateful nor thankful for our help, we should concentrate on our nation's needs, our infrastructure, creating attractive investment opportunities in the process. We should also return our government to fiscal responsibility and our own citizens to self-reliance, not handouts and entitled cradle-to-grave welfare.

Who Controls the Price of Oil?

Most people do not understand what drives the price of oil but readily accept the explanation pushed by this administration that it is the unbounded greed of oil companies and their "fat cat owners." Oil companies are publicly traded and many Americans and other foreign nationals or entities can own stock or bonds in these firms.

Most economists agree that the oil industry is an oligopoly, a market dominated by a few sellers, synonymous in developed countries with "big business." An insidious form of oligopoly, which dominates the oil industry, is the cartel. The cartel's firms join forces to control production, sale, and the price of oil.

OPEC, the most notable and successful cartel, controls 44 percent of the world's crude oil production and 79 percent of world's crude oil reserves. By restricting output, its members, Algeria, Angola, Ecuador, Iran, Iraq, Kuwait, Libya, Nigeria, Qatar, Saudi Arabia, United Arab Emirates and Venezuela, quadrupled the price of oil between 1973-1974 and 1979-1980.

OPEC should not be able to burden consumers to the same extent now because large oil reserves were discovered in Alaska, North Sea, Canada, and the Gulf of Mexico. However our business-killing EPA regulations, the killing of the Keystone XL pipeline from Canada, and Obama's seven-year moratorium on drilling in the Gulf do.

When oligopolists organize themselves in a successful cartel such as OPEC, prices will be higher and outputs lower. Cartels are illegal in the U.S. even though some companies such as railroad and gas pipeline transportation behave like cartels under regulations that prevent firms from undercutting prices.

According to the Wall Street Journal, Exxon's margin of profit for both oil and gas ranks #60. There are 59 more profitable industries than the oil industry. Oil and gas firms profit 8 cents per dollar of sales. Pharmaceuticals profit 20 cents and banks profit 18 cents per dollar of sales.

According to the Report to Congress made in April 2008 called "Oil Industry and Profit Review," the factors contributing to high gas prices were:
- World unrest
- Increases in the price of crude oil that pushed the spot price of West Texas Intermediate (a key oil price in determining market prices)
- Tight market conditions
- Demand growth in China, India and other parts of the developing world
- Political unrest in Nigeria, Venezuela, Iraq, Iran, Lybia and other parts of the world
- The decline of the value of the U.S. dollar on world currency markets
- Investment strategies of financial firms on the oil futures markets
- Volatility of the world oil and financial markets

The refining segment of the market performed relatively poorly during the same period. According to the U.S. Energy Information Administration, there are 148 operable refineries in the U.S., down from 150 in 2009. Only 137 refineries are actually operating, down from 141 in 2009. Eleven refineries are idle for various reasons. The atmospheric crude oil distilling capacity is 16,937,024 barrels per calendar day of actually operating refineries.

We have not built new refineries in the U.S. in the past 25 years. The last refinery built was in Garyville, Louisiana and it started in 1976. In the mid-1970s, a refinery construction was proposed in Portsmouth, Virginia. The company canceled the project in 1984 after a nine-year court battle with environmentalists. Even if we drilled more, we could not refine the excess supply of crude.

There are three reasons why oil refineries are not built:
- refineries are not particularly profitable
- environmentalists fight planning and construction every step of the way
- government red tape makes the task almost impossible

According to Investor's Business Daily, the cost of building a new refinery is $2-$4 billion. Twenty billion dollars have to be dedicated over a ten-year period to reducing the sulphur content in gasoline. Diesel is even more costly to produce since almost every drop of sulphur must be extracted, making its production more expensive than gasoline. Additionally, 800 different permits have to be collected. The long-term rate of return on capital is just 5 percent.

"I'm sure that at some point in the last 20 years someone has considered building a new refinery," says James Halloran, an energy analyst with National City Corp. "But they quickly came to their senses."

The current administration keeps pushing the euphemism "green energy" although there are no plans in the foreseeable future for such affordable energy. Any hybrid or electric car uses electricity generated with fossil fuels, including the maligned coal, which the president promised to put out of business. The electric Volt is only popular with the die-hard leftists.

Today's oil prices are twice as high as they were in 2008 and nine times as high as they were in 1998. The price of oil also hinges on the perceived replacement cost of the next barrel of oil and nobody is quite sure what that price will be.

In Canada, it costs $40-$60 per barrel to extract the oil from the sands. It costs Chevron $15 per barrel to deep drill crude from the Gulf of Mexico. It is even cheaper in the Middle East. The political and physical risk of extracting the oil in war zones is even higher.

The volatility factor depends on the volatility of our economy. None of Obama's economic stimuli have worked. In March, during intense fighting in Libya, he said that there was no supply shortage and rising oil prices was not a good reason to tap reserves. He changed his mind on June 23, when he released oil from our Strategic Petroleum Reserves under the excuse of turmoil in Libya. Again, it was a failed economic stimulus.

Christina Romer, former White House chief economic advisor, told an audience that we were in a "growth-less recovery." Recovery without growth may exist in a fantasy world - the patient is flat-lined but somehow still alive.

Republicans and big business blame Obama's drilling moratorium for the oil price problem. Democrats blame "speculators" on the Chicago Board of Trade for soaring gas prices, particularly Goldman Sachs whose influential analysts move all markets.

The Commodity Futures Trading Commission investigated manipulation when the price of natural gas dropped 8 percent in 14 seconds in after-hour trading. The commission charged two traders with swindling $50 million in profits by manipulating oil markets in 2008.

"They bought physical cargoes they did not need to artificially inflate prices while also buying derivatives so they would profit as the prices rose. They bought other derivatives that would pay off later when the prices fell – which they did after they sold the physical barrels, catching other traders off guard."

Attempting to corner a piece of the market is illegal but can warp prices for a short period, resulting in higher prices for consumers.

Current world supply can also be an expression of consumption growth in China and India by more than half a million barrels of oil per day. There is a world spare capacity of 3-4 million of barrels of oil per day, which can shrink, with more consumption growth, thus resulting in higher prices.

Liberals believe that supplies should be rationed through deliberate higher prices in order to protect the planet from unnecessary pollution. They are not concerned that it would stifle economic growth. Their main concern is how it would affect the re-election of Obama. To prevent a re-election loss, Democrats want to release more strategic reserves into the market in order to keep the gas price lower at the pump and thus please the voters.

Who Stole Your 401K, Savings, and Taxpayer TARP

Short selling is a legal form of stock buying when you borrow shares you do not own from your broker, sell them, and pocket the money. When the price of that stock drops, you buy the number of shares at the lower price and return them to the broker, plus interest and commission, and you keep the difference. When you buy the shares back, you have covered the short position.

The risks are as follows:

- the stock could go up instead of down
- the drop in price may take a long time (Timing is important since you are paying the broker interest.)
- if the stock goes up more than you made from short-selling the stock, you will be forced to pay more to cover your short position

Selling short tends to increase when the market is booming. Short sellers believe that a correction is due, a drop in price, especially if the economy does not seem to grow as fast as stock prices are rising.

The Securities and Exchange Commission (SEC) rule states that if a company has had at least 550,000 shares sold short or a change of short interest of at least 250,000 in the month, it must report the daily average volume of shares sold short.

The names of the companies with the largest short positions and the greatest change are tracked, as well as the recent history of short interest. The short interest ratio explains the number of days it would take to cover the short interest in selected stocks if trading continued.

Short sellers can be caught in a squeeze. A stock that has been heavily shorted begins to rise. Short sellers scramble to cover their short positions, resulting in heavy buying, thus driving up the price even higher.

A former rule established by the SEC required that every short sale transaction be entered at a price that is higher than the price of the previous trade. This rule was introduced in the Securities Exchange Act of 1934 as Rule 10a-1 and was implemented in 1938. The "uptick rule" prevents short sellers from adding to the downward momentum when the price of an asset is already experiencing sharp declines.

The uptick or "plus tick rule" was formulated in 1938 to regulate short selling of stocks and was eliminated on July 6, 2007. The uptick rule simply states that a stock cannot be sold short unless the sale price is above the last sold price. The previous sale price can be matched if it is higher than the preceding sale price.

Short sellers want prices to fall and their sales help those prices to fall. By only allowing short sellers to sell during price rises (when they'd rather not sell), the uptick rule helps to eliminate the recurring cycle of falling prices leading to more short sales leading to even lower prices and more short sales. The effectiveness of the uptick rule is debatable, detractors say, it is largely the reason it was eliminated under SEC Chairman Christopher Cox. Proponents claim, the uptick rule's dismissal exacerbated the financial crisis in 2008. The existence of the uptick rule helped the market recover after the Great Depression.

"The Glass-Steagall Act, also known as the Banking Act of 1933 (48 Stat. 162), was passed by Congress in 1933 and prohibits commercial banks from engaging in the investment business" thus in risky trading activities.

Named after Carter Glass and Henry Steagall, "It was enacted as an emergency response to the failure of nearly 5,000 banks during the Great Depression. The act was originally part of President Franklin D. Roosevelt's *New Deal* program and became a permanent measure in 1945. It gave tighter regulation of national banks to the Federal Reserve System; prohibited bank sales of securities; and created the Federal Deposit Insurance Corporation (FDIC), which insures bank deposits with a pool of money appropriated from banks." (The New York Times)

President Obama's Glass-Steagall act for the 21st century is the *"Volcker rule"* named after former Federal Reserve Chairman Paul Volcker. This act aims to stop banks that take deposits from running hedge funds, making private equity investments, using their money to take bets on markets, and stop big mergers between banks.

Glass-Steagall forced commercial and investment banks to separate. Commercial banks were not allowed to underwrite sales of stocks and bonds, while investment banks could not take in deposits from customers.

Glass-Steagall was repealed in 1999 through the Financial Services Modernization Act, promoted by Gramm, Leach, and Bliley. The Republicans who repealed this act allowed banks to retail, invest, and become insurance companies. This law is widely blamed for the financial crisis that created the financial bubble in 2008 and TARP.

The U.S. taxpayers were forced to bail out Wall Street including several large foreign banks headquartered in Europe and the AIG insurance giant. AIG creditors did not take a loss, the Treasury paid them in full with taxpayer dollars.

The U.S. taxpayers were forced to bail out Citigroup. If the law had not been changed in 1999, Citigroup would not have been allowed to exist after Citibank announced the intention to merge with the insurance giant, Travelers.

Another safeguard to investors removed on November 15, 2007, was conventional accounting standards; it was replaced with market-to-market accounting standards. Conventional accounting valued assets at the price at which they were acquired. Market-to-market accounting valued assets at the price at which they could be sold currently. (Michael Savage – Trickle Up Poverty)

Each day, if the value of assets declined, the holder of assets had to produce cash to offset the decline. Banks had to find quick cash in order to offset the decline in values. This created a liquidity problem that finally led to the Troubled Asset Relief Program (TARP), a $787 billion bailout of foreign and domestic financial institutions. The panic was in place, stoked by politicians, the Secretary of the Treasury Paulson and the Federal Reserve Chairman Bernanke. Americans lost $10 trillion in 401k, investments, and retirement accounts, a decisive turn in favoring a Democrat candidate and electing a progressive President. From October 2007 to November 2008, the Dow Jones lost from 14,000 points to almost half of its value.

Americans soon learned they've been cheated financially. On May 6, 2010, the Dow dropped almost 1,000 points in a few minutes. The media excused it that some trader added too many zeroes to the shares sold, while others blamed it on Greece's economic situation in the EU.

Some economists blamed the short sellers since the drop occurred after 2:30 p.m. when there was no safety mechanism in place to halt trading if the Dow dropped 10 percent. Had it happened before 2:30 p.m., the Dow's computers would have automatically shut down. Days earlier, this "alternative" uptick rule (halting the trade if the market drops 10 percent before 2:30 p.m. but not afterwards) had been put in place by the new SEC Chairwoman, Mary Shapiro. (Michael Savage – Trickle Up Poverty)

Hedge fund traders clearly controlled the market. Short sellers drove the price of many stocks so low, some down to a penny, then bought them back, drove the market back up and made close to a trillion dollars in the process.

Hedge funds are not bound by the same rules as mutual funds. In addition to short selling a stock, hedge funds can trade in derivatives, "financial instruments based on things such as mortgages that are designed to reduce the risk associated with owning the underlying securities." (Nelson D. Schwartz and Louise Story) Bad mortgages were usually bundled with good mortgages and sold as a financial instrument to a third party.

When John McCain had asked for Christopher Cox's resignation and stated, "we have no tolerance for naked short selling," it was already too late, the damage had been done, in spite of the fact that the uptick rule had been reinstated in February 2010 and market-to-market accounting relaxed in March 2009.

The Managed Fund Association (MFA), a group of hedge fund investors, was believed to have lobbied the SEC to change the rules in order to engineer a financial meltdown whose victims were Lehmann Brothers, Wachovia, and the American taxpayers. Hedge fund owners, traders and an inexperienced candidate to the highest and most powerful office in the world were the victors. (Michael Savage – Trickle Up Poverty)

Some economists and many Americans believe that the Managed Fund Association, the Federal Reserve Board, and Wall Street answer financially to higher powers, the Bildeberger Group, the Trilateral Commission, and the Council on Foreign Relations, whose ultimate goals are to install a one-world government with the help of United Nation's Agenda 21.

As we now know, the Lehman's bankruptcy caused a run-on-banks by panicked investors who wanted to withdraw their cash. Paulson and Bernanke convinced most politicians and the public that TARP was not just necessary but the only solution to our gloom and doom.

TARP was not necessary and it was not a wise move. Unsound financial institutions should have been allowed to fail. The "too big to fail" mantra turned from a big lie into another manufactured emergency that placed the American people into deeper and unnecessary debt.

Unions Are the Political Dinosaur in the Room

A famous radio talk show host asked rhetorically why unions have supported and financed the Occupy Wall Street movement. The answer is quite simple. Occupiers are asking for communism. In communism, the entire labor force is unionized. It is in the best interest of unions to promote communism since union membership in this country is down to single digits and not likely to rebound.

Unions were necessary at the turn of the 20th century to protect workers from dangerous working conditions. Unions survive today as a political tool to influence elections and exert economic power.

Otto von Bismarck introduced the first welfare system in Prussia in 1883 which provided workers with sick days, workman's compensation, and retirement benefits. He disliked trade unions and, in order to reduce their socialist influence, Bismarck introduced workplace compensation.

The Triangle Shirtwaist Factory Fire of 1911 in New York turned public opinion behind the union movement to improve working conditions, hours, and wages in sweatshops.

Pauline Newman, an organizer and executive of the newly formed International Ladies Garment Workers' Union, worked in the Triangle Factory at the tender age of eight. "We didn't have anything… There was no welfare, no pension, and no unemployment insurance. There was nothing…There was so much feeling against unions then. One hundred and forty-six people perished in the fire while the judge fined Blank and Harris seventy-five dollars."

Unions started gaining track as more accidents were exposed and workers demanded protection. Union membership enrolled by 1930 slightly less than 7 percent of the U.S. labor force. In the 1950s, 26 percent of the labor force was unionized. Currently, less than 9 percent of all employees belong to a union.

The drop in union membership can be attributed to the switch from manufacturing, in which unions are predominant, to the service industry. Deregulation in airline industry and trucking forced fiercer competition. Firms downsized, closing plants, moving them overseas in response to unions demanding higher wages and more benefits. The decline in union membership in the U.S. is also a function of American rugged individualism, conservatism, and hostility towards unions. Factories have moved from northern states to the southern states where unions are not so popular.

Union membership levels in the U.S. are much lower than Germany's (30 percent), Sweden's (80 percent), Denmark's and Finland's (70 percent). Belgium's and Norway's (50 percent), Ireland's (40 percent), Italy's and Austria's (30 percent), U.K's, Netherlands' and Switzerland's (20 percent). (OECD data)

Government employment has large numbers of union members (37 percent). This begs the question why is it necessary for government workers to protect themselves against the general public. The private sector employees who earn much less than public employees must pay for the generous union salaries and benefits via confiscatory taxes. If they refuse, the public employees strike and create mayhem as we have seen in Wisconsin.

A union is a labor monopoly. As it struggles to survive, it must find new members among non-traditional sectors such as agriculture and white-collar office markets. Unions have organized teachers and government employees quite successfully.

U.S. unions are different from European or Japanese unions because they operate as adversaries to management. Japanese unions engage in labor-management cooperation. European labor unions tend to be socialist. SEIU in the U.S. openly promotes and supports socialism through groups like Occupy Wall Street and ACORN.

Countries like Germany with a rate of 30 percent unionization prefer cooperation to adversarial relationships between labor and management. According to Horst Mund, head of IG Metall, "workers in the auto industry have high wages and excellent working conditions for two reasons. Virtually all workers are unionized members of IG Metall, the German autoworkers' union, yielding power to keep wages high. They have the right to strike but they do not because there is an elaborate system of conflict resolution. The German Constitution includes a second mechanism for keeping employees involved in the decisions of the firm for which they work."

It is illegal to strike in some states when the private interest of an employee may harm the public interest such as striking by teachers, nurses, traffic controllers, or doctors. In 1981, Ronald Reagan fired all 13,000 striking traffic controllers who refused to return to work.

Some economists estimate that most union members' wages are about 20 percent higher than salaries of non-members who have identical skills, education, and geographical location. The non-monetary benefits are often overlooked in remuneration calculations.

Public sector workers have "defined benefits" such as pensions which provide guaranteed income based on career length and peak salaries, generous retiree health insurance coverage, and job security.

A New York public school teacher earns $100,000 and can retire at 55 with a pension of $60,000. A private sector employee would need savings of $1.2 million to buy an annuity with the same yield, starting at the same young age. (Manhattan Institute's Empire Center)

A city police officer collects $70,563 plus lavish health benefits and is able to retire in his forties. Few private employees have so much money saved that they can match public benefits. "According to the Federal Reserve, the average worker in his late fifties, has a balance of $85,600 in his retirement account, and a net worth of $222,300 overall." (Lawrence Mone)

"New York City pension's costs have jumped from about 4 percent of city tax revenues to 20 percent over the past decade, crowding out other vital public investments." Taxpayers are worried about union compensation and unfunded pension liabilities. Lawrence Mone calls these public employees "municipal millionaires."

Voters in Ohio foolishly renewed this year the largesse towards the union salaries and benefits, agreeing to pay higher taxes in order to supply their fellow citizens with Cadillac health insurance plans and other benefits.

According to the Heritage Foundation, "Government employee unions are the largest special interest group in the country. Government unions spend more than any other outside group on U.S. elections." Of the top five political spenders, three are unions: *American Federation of State, County, and Municipal Employees* ($91 million), *Service Employees International Union* ($44 million), and *National Education Association* ($40 million).

Union members pay dues but they have little say in how their dues are spent even though the Supreme Court decision *Communication Workers v. Beck* (1988) stated that "workers cannot be forced to donate to political causes, and are entitled to demand a refund of the portion of their dues spent on politics."

Unions engage in curious activities such as funding a credit union almost entirely by one local union chapter, with most loans going to four people. Nepotism created a bogus job ($119,000 per year) with the sole purpose to manage a scholarship fund that awarded $28,000 per year. A board member's daughter earned $112,000 per year as a "confidential secretary" to listen to voice mail messages; she checked 109 messages in one year. United Auto Workers created trust funds to retrain laid-off workers and spent the money sponsoring NASCAR racers, a "Hollywood Showcase" at the 2000 Democrat Convention, and lavish conventions in Las Vegas. (Heritage Foundation)

Government unions control public policy through donations, serving their interests and not those of the general public by putting pressure on policy makers. TSA and Homeland Security should not be allowed to engage in limited collective bargaining because their number one priority must be the interests of American citizens.

Unions organized through secret ballots. Joining a union through "card-check" would harass and pressure workers to make public information they wish to keep private. The Employee Free Choice Act would prohibit the private ballot and the "check card" system would be used in favor of unions and in disfavor of the employer and the employees.

Unions discourage productivity; they are "anti-individualist movements and the epitome of socialism." Marginal union employees receive tenure and cannot be fired without a lengthy and expensive termination process. The overall cost of doing business is higher and such costs are always passed on to the consumer. Employees are obligated by unions to pay dues, cannot opt out, and have no voice in how the money is spent. The Unions' abundant financial resources have gone into the electoral coffers of the Democrat Party.

Union employees no longer have the incentive to excel or compete as the union protection makes them complacent. Unions see illegal immigrants as a threat to their pay scale since immigrants are willing to work for lower pay.

Union workers in the U.S. complain that they can earn as much as workers in France, Germany, and Denmark but they have to work almost three months longer.

American workers bemoan the fact that they do not receive six weeks paid vacation in their first year of employment, paid maternity leave, higher and longer unemployment compensation, and universal health care like the Europeans. What they fail to mention, however, is that most of these governments are spending huge portions of their GDP on social programs, while the U.S. is providing them with free financial support through the IMF, military support, protection, and security for Europe. They also fail to mention the fact that European universal health care is a disaster, rationed, substandard to the U.S., and grossly negligent with little or no malpractice responsibility.

Unions can directly constrain the number of workers that can enter a specific trade or company and indirectly, by pressuring employers to increase wages. Unions thus have a negative impact on jobs for those outside of the union.

Unions represent their members legally but the rest of the workers do not have a legal voice. Management often prefers not to have anyone from the labor union team on their staff. Promotions are thus hindered by union membership.

When the Department of Labor was created in 1913, historical records stated that "it was the direct product of a half-century campaign by organized labor for a voice in the Cabinet." This voice has become today an indirect advocate for socialism.

All federally-financed or assisted construction projects costs are more expensive because of the existence of the Davis-Bacon Act of 1931 which requires companies to pay "prevailing wages." A prevailing wage is a union-level wage. The Davis-Bacon Act added almost $11 billion to federal construction costs in 2011. "Suspending the law would employ 155,000 additional workers in the process." (Heritage Foundation)

"An executive order from President Obama strongly encourages federal agencies to use project labor agreements (PLAs) on federal construction projects. A PLA requires contractors to sign a collective bargaining agreement with construction unions before beginning work. This executive order discriminates against the 87 percent of construction workers who do not belong to unions." Construction costs are 12-18 percent higher because of union labor only hires.

The National Labor Relations Board is reinterpreting labor laws under President Obama because the National Labor Relations Act was drafted carelessly. The act outlaws efforts to "interfere with, restrain, or coerce employees," but Congress did not define these terms.

NLRB sued Boeing through the International Association of Machinists (IAM). IAM organized strikes all the time, costing Boeing billions of dollars. Boeing built a new 787 airliner assembly line in South

Carolina, a right-to-work state. NLRB claimed, it was an unfair labor practice and wanted to force Boeing to relocate its nearly finished plant to Washington in order to give union members first preference for new jobs.

The Norris-La Guardia Act of 1932 changed labor laws in order to strengthen the power of labor unions. The National Labor Relations Act (Wagner Act) of 1935 determined the structure of private-sector unions in the U.S. and promoted equality of bargaining power between employers and employees. These acts served the interests of union labor rather than the interests of all labor. The national right-to-work law is necessary because no worker should be forced to join, or pay dues, to a labor union.

British policemen, French rail workers, Greek civil servants, and teachers' unions strained the budgets of the cash-strapped European Union. Private sector has experienced a severe union membership drop but the public sector is strong. Over half of workers in Britain are unionized. Most civil servants in continental Europe belong to unions. "Many center-left parties are union-backed. Britain's Labor Party gets 80 percent of its funding from public sector unions. Spain's sluggish state reform may be partly explained by its prime minister's union membership." (The Economist)

The National Education Association (NEA) had one tenth of the delegates who attended the Democrat National Convention. The British Medical Association's vested interests were defended by "nice middle-class women." According to the Economist, Singapore had the best civil service in the world and some of its workers were paid $2 million a year.

The European unionized worker's pay is excellent but the benefits are absurd. Holidays, vacations, and pension are beyond generous. Many can retire in mid-fifties with full pay. It is insane to pay such retirements when governments are broke. Over 600 professions in Greece allow workers to retire at 55.

"Public wages and pension payments absorb half of the Greek national budget. The government does not know how many people are in the civil service, since that would require competence. It is now undertaking a census of civil servants. The guess is that it's about one-in-three people. The constitution guarantees these jobs for life." Public sector workers pay has doubled in the past ten years in Greece. Workers get bonuses of two extra months' pay annually regardless of performance. "(Real Clear Politics)

According to the Cato Institute, Greece's debt is 875 percent of GDP when pension obligations are included. When Social Security and Medicare unfunded liabilities are considered, U.S. debt is 500 percent of GDP. And that does not factor in Obamacare.

Given the history of unions in the last 100 years, what would the impact be if all unions faded away? Would all manufacturing stop, would workers be exploited, would the teachers not get paid fair wages? Would policemen and firemen not have pensions? Would labor rights and advancements be lost? Would workers be mistreated? Would it affect the European or American debt crisis? I think not. The time for unions is over; they have run their course and usefulness. Unions are the political dinosaur in the room, the 8-track in the dust bin of history.

Labor Unions, GE, and the Job Czar

In a free market economy, no single wage level applies to all workers. In general, wage differentials are determined by the fact that we have many labor markets, each with its own supply and demand and equilibrium wage.

Each worker in a specific labor market has certain ability and expends a degree of effort commensurate with their ability and work ethic. Other factors of production make American workers more productive because they have generous supplies of machinery, natural resources, and technical expertise. Therefore, they earn higher wages. Some workers have a superior education, training, and experience.

The size of the available working population explains the magnitude or dearth of industrial activity. Sparsely populated Alaska experienced high wages when the Alaskan oil pipeline created many jobs, while wages in Appalachia remain low.

The nonmonetary attractiveness of a job explains why pleasant and self-satisfying jobs, such as teaching, attract many workers and pay a relatively low wage. Disagreeable and dangerous jobs, such as working with gunpowder or mining, command higher wages.

Some workers receive economic rent for their unique abilities that few people can duplicate, such as a famous surgeon, athlete, or actor. Their wages will have a component to the pay that does not reflect necessarily the amount of labor hours.

Investment in education or human capital is also a variable in wage differentials. It is the perceived incorrect opinion that an educated person will make a better worker.

Doctors and lawyers earn such high salaries partly because of their many years of training and financial investment in their human capital, time, tuition and books. They have to eschew any part-time work for years in order to study for very difficult classes and exams. The years that they do not work, is income lost that cannot be recovered in the future.

Education theorists assume that students in high schools and colleges acquire skills that make them more productive and knowledgeable. Experience tells us that is not necessarily the case. Some are more willing to learn than others are, but are not necessarily productive. People with higher education earn more money but there is definitive disagreement among experts as to why they do.

The dual labor market has the primary "good jobs" market with the possibility of promotion and the secondary "bad jobs" market with little hope for advancement. Increased education leads to promotion in the first tier while more education in the second tier offers little hope for promotion.

In many labor markets, the supply of labor is not competitive because it is controlled by labor unions and collective bargaining, a form of monopoly. Less than 9 percent of the labor force is now unionized; the decline was caused by the diminishing manufacturing base and the move to a service economy.

Unions, as monopoly sellers of labor, have the power to push wages above the competitive level in the marketplace. Unions and management settle on the terms of a labor contract through a process called collective bargaining: mediation, arbitration, and strikes.

Outsourcing and cheap foreign labor, in spite of the economists denial, have hurt American manufacturing base and American workers. Consumers, however, have benefitted greatly and so did the Chinese, other foreign workers, and their respective economies, built on the destruction of our industrial base and reverse engineering.

National Labor Relations Board (NLRB) was established by Executive Order 6763 on June 29, 1934 and was formed on July 5, 1935. In 2008, it had 1,628 employees.

The National Labor Relations Board (NLRB) is an "independent agency of the U.S. government charged with conducting elections for labor union representation and with investigating and remedying unfair labor practices. Unfair labor practices may involve union-related situations or instances of protected concerted activity."

The NLRB is governed by a five-person board and a General Counsel, all appointed by the President with Senate consent. Board members are appointed to five-year terms and the General Counsel is appointed to a four-year term. The General Counsel acts as a prosecutor and the Board acts as an appellate judicial body from decisions of administrative law judges.

In April 2011, NLRB filed a complaint "seeking to force Boeing to bring an airplane production line back to its unionized facilities in Washington State instead of moving the work to a nonunion plant in South Carolina."

Companies have taken advantage of the "right to work" rules in most Southern states to relocate there without fear of work stoppages at every turn. Any company should have the right to locate their business where they feel it is in their best interest. Apparently, the government disagrees when union employees are employed in another state.

Boeing transferred a second production line of its 787 Dreamliner plane to South Carolina; they were accused of unlawful retaliation against union workers for their past strikes in Washington and discouraging future strikes. NLRB acting general counsel, Lafe Solomon, said it was "illegal for companies to take actions in retaliation against workers for exercising the right to strike."

President's appointees at NLRB "have declared open season on Right to Work states, independent workers, and job providers like the Boeing Company."

The saga continues with a "quickie or ambush election rule" that would shorten the time for union elections from a median 38 days to as little as 10. The stacked deck in favor of unions would:

- Deny employees adequate time to make informed decisions on whether to join a union
- Silence employers from expressing their views on unionization to employee
- Push Big Labor's radical agenda

Wisconsin's Governor Scott Walker waged a battle with labor unions in his attempt to balance the state's budget. Wisconsin had public collective bargaining rights since 1959 and employees had very generous benefits. I would never understand why public employees need protection from the public, essentially themselves. They simply expected other workers in the state to pay for their Cadillac health care plans, benefits, generous salaries, and retirement pay.

After a three week standoff during which massive union and Democrat forces from across the country caused millions of dollars in damage to the State's Capitol, the 14 Democrat Senators fled the state in order to deny a quorum vote to pass a budget measure, the Republicans outmaneuvered them, and the law was passed.

A recent update proves that some school districts in Wisconsin are now showing a surplus instead of a deficit. It seems that the insurance company that provided all the benefits to the teachers was owned and operated by the teacher's union.

The insurance was guaranteed to get the teacher's business and the State had to pay for it, not the teachers. The insurance would increase the annual costs every single year, to become the most expensive insurance in the state. In turn, the insurance company would donate millions of dollars to their favorite Democrat politician. Once elected, the politicians kept funding the unions' outrageous costs.

General Electric transferred its X-ray machine operations from Waukesha, Wisconsin to China. The 100-year old business will "tap emerging market growth." "The move follows the introduction earlier this year of GE Healthcare "Spring Wind" initiative to develop and distribute medical products and services in China," GE said in a statement.

GE is the biggest maker of MRI and CT scanners and sold $1.1 billion of its $16.9 billion in China last year. GE will hire 65 new engineers and support staff at the new Chengdu facility. GE has already hired a "large number" of engineers who are in training.

GE will invest $2 billion across China, including opening six "customer innovation and development centers." Is this a good idea since we have such high unemployment here in the U.S.? Are they using taxpayer dollars when we are broke and are debating default v. raising the debt ceiling by borrowing another trillion dollars from China?

Considering that Mr. Immelt, General Electric's CEO is our Jobs Czar, does it not seem bizarre that he is killing jobs in the U.S. and creating jobs in China? Is this punishment for Governor Walker winning the fight in Wisconsin against Big Labor?

Green Jobs Debacle

Sifting through Congressional records is tedious work. I wanted to find out for myself how a half a billion-taxpayer dollars were spent with the American Recovery and Reinvestment Act of 2009, which was earmarked to fund employment and training programs for Americans.

The unemployment rate was abysmal yet the Employment Training Administration (ETA) received half a billion dollars in grants for research, labor exchange, and job training projects for careers in renewable energy industries and energy efficiency, the administration's so-called "Green Jobs" program. Where were the jobs?

The Department of Labor's Office of Inspector General (OIG), an independent entity, was asked by Congress to audit this Green Jobs program. The Inspector General's office was told to find out how ETA defined "green jobs," how ETA used the half billion dollars, how much training and placement workers received, and what was their job retention rate. The findings were a typical example of government waste of taxpayer dollars.

"Green jobs" were defined as "jobs associated with products and services that use renewable energy resources, reduce pollution, and conserve natural resources. This is nothing new, since such jobs were defined in the Occupational Information Network and more recently in the Energy Policy Act of 2005 and the Green Jobs Act of 2007, long before the current presidency.

The half billion dollars were awarded as grants to 189 entities, mostly for training programs and $54.7 million for non-training programs. Program administration and technical assistance swallowed the remaining $9.9 million.

Twenty-five projects, mostly first time recipients of grants, prepared and placed workers for "green jobs" such as hybrid/electric auto technicians, weatherization specialists (caulkers), and solar panel installers.

Thirty-eight grants were distributed to Pathways Out of Poverty projects ($147.7 million) for worker recruitment, job referral services, basic skills, work-readiness, occupational skills training, and supportive services to overcome barriers to employment. Non-profit agencies, community colleges, and State Workforce Agencies received the funds. I am translating this as another redistribution of wealth scheme to support the current administration's goals.

Non-training programs squandered $54.7 million to disseminate "green jobs" information through State Labor Markets, to help workers find jobs after training, equipment purchases, curriculum development, and hiring of additional staff.

The audit found that all the money had been allocated as of June 30, 2011. Only 33 percent of the grants were spent, the entire sum was already obligated to be spent in the future, but 73 percent of the training and non-training periods had already elapsed. The money was spent but only some training took place. So much for government efficiency and use of taxpayer dollars.

Forty-two percent of the recipients were trained. Twenty-seven percent had completed training. Only ten percent of participants entered employment and only TWO percent had retained employment for more than six months. This is a monumental waste of half a billion dollars. Even ETA acknowledged that grant recipients complained that the overall economic conditions were poor and green jobs had not materialized.

"ETA could not demonstrate that grantees were on target to meet grant outcomes nor was there a plan to ensure that they could."

Elliot P. Lewis, Assistant Inspector General for Audit, testified to the House Committee on Oversight and Government Reform on November 2, 2011 that OIG is "concerned as to whether grantees will effectively use the funds and deliver targeted employment outcomes by the end of the grant periods."

It is a false statement to say that there is high demand for "green job-related skills." The OIG audit recommended that "ETA evaluate the Green Jobs program and obtain a current estimate of the funds each grantee will realistically spend given the current job market and the demand for green job-related skills."

Unfortunately the taxpayers lost half a billion dollars because ETA had obligated all of its Recovery Act funds, "and it expects that all funds will have been expended by September 30, 2013, as required by the Office of Management and Budget."

The Green Energy debacle has washed down the proverbial drain another half billion dollars with no visible success or green jobs "created or saved," to use a favorite expression of this administration.

Green Energy Not Ready for Prime Time

G. K. Chesterton (1874-1936), a prolific English writer, said, "The whole world has divided itself into Conservatives and Progressives. The business of Progressives is to go on making mistakes. The business of Conservatives is to prevent mistakes from being corrected."

As our President promised to "double down" on renewable energy, in spite of the bankrupted Solyndra, three more green energy companies, recipients of stimulus dollars, have collapsed.

Evergreen Energy Inc., a developer of alternative fuel products, filed Chapter 7 bankruptcy in a Delaware court on January 23, 2012. Chapter 7 bankruptcy allows the company to liquidate its assets while being protected from creditors. Evergreen Inc. has $25 million in debt and $240 million in assets. Without further financing, the company cannot continue to operate its K-Fuel facility in China. K-Fuel is a process of "refining coal before it is burned to increase energy densities and combustion efficiencies which reduce greenhouse gas emissions."

Solyndra LLC (solar panel maker) and Beacon Power Corporation (energy storage) filed for bankruptcy last year after receiving government loan guarantees.

Solyndra received $535 million in government loan guarantees and listed in its bankruptcy papers $854.1 million in assets and $867.1 million in debt.

Beacon had $72 million in assets and $47 million debt. Beacon had built a $69 million power plant in New York with U.S. Department of Energy loans.

Ener1 Inc., a manufacturer of lithium-ion batteries for electric cars, filed Chapter 11 bankruptcy in Manhattan claiming heavy competition from Toyota, China, and Korea, and the demise of a major customer, Norway Think Global. Ener1 had received $118.5 million grant from the Department of Energy. The company has $73.9 million in assets and $90.5 million in debt.

Amonix, Inc., a manufacturer of solar panels that received $5.9 billion in stimulus money will cut 200 employees, seven months after opening a factory in Nevada. (Las Vegas Sun)

It appears that producing clean, renewable energy is not such a cheap and affordable proposition after all. In spite of the green movement's desire to replace "dirty" fossil fuels at all costs, it is not economically feasible to do so at this time.

In addition, the bad news mounts for the progressives who want to send us back to the Stone Age with their global warming fear mongering. The faux "consensus" that global warming is man-made was challenged again by newly released temperature data showing that earth has not warmed in the past 15 years. The temperature readings came from 30,000 measuring stations.

The infamous University of East Anglia Climactic Research Unit and the Met Office confirmed, "The rising trend in world temperatures ended in 1997." (Daily Mail)

As various scientists compare and contrast diverse methods of climate modeling that take into account the influence of solar flares and the significance of CO_2 emissions, it is evident that there were severe shortcomings and misrepresentations in the theories, data, and readings advanced by progressives.

Leading climate scientists believe that the sun will no longer emit high levels of energy as it did in the 20th century and will deliver a "grand minimum" of output, opening the possibility of colder summers, very cold winters, and much shorter growing seasons for food. (The Mail)

Some scientists, however, are still very confident that "solar activity is insufficient to offset the dominant influence of greenhouse gases."

"World temperatures may wind up a lot cooler than now for 50 years or more. It will take a long battle to convince some climate scientists that the sun is important. It may well be that the sun is going to demonstrate this on its own, without the need for their help." (Henrik Svensmark, Director, Center for Sun-Climate Research at Denmark's National Space Institute)

One can only conclude that the global warming alarm was manufactured based on insufficient or deliberately misrepresented data. The progressives marched on with their agenda to replace traditional fossil fuel energy sources with a non-existent green renewable energy industry, which bankrupted itself in a short time, and the conservatives did nothing to stop them.

Obama's Six Agency Merger – Smoke and Mirrors

The President has decided, after spending trillions of dollars, that it was time for an "effective, lean government." Like most of the promises he made, the intention is suspect. He wants Congress to give him greater power to merge six major economic agencies into one.

The six departments in question are the Commerce Department, the Export-Import Bank, the Office of U.S. Trade Representative, the Overseas Private Investment Corporation, the Small Business Administration, and the U.S. Trade and Development Agency.

To support his move, Obama uses a bizarre quote to exemplify government inefficiency. "The Interior Department is in charge of salmon while they're in fresh water, but the Commerce Department handles them when they're in saltwater. And I hear it gets even more complicated once they're smoked."

For starters, the Interior Department is not in question. The administration says that 1,000 to 1,200 jobs would be cut through attrition and the merger would save $3 billion dollars over ten years.

Considering the out-of-control spending this administration has engaged in the last three years, $300 million a year is a drop in the bucket. It is more about "smoke and mirrors," a political attempt to help the Obama re-election by portraying him as an advocate for a lean and effective government.

Combining organizations is not about simplifying government but the political appearance of reducing the size of government. The move is tied to Obama's National Export Initiative (NEI) and the Executive Order of March 2010. The Senate did not fund the NEI in the 2012 Commerce Appropriation. He thinks Congress will fund his NEI if it appears that he is streamlining his outlandish spending.

The National Export Initiative (NEI) is a plan that he unveiled in the 2010 State of the Union address. Obama promised to "double U.S. exports over the next five years and support 2 million American jobs" by creating an export promotion cabinet (to oversee government programs and special financing for farmers seeking overseas market opportunities) and tougher enforcement of international trade laws.

Congress is also resisting reauthorization of the Export-Import Bank. It is my opinion that a bank should remain independent of a six-organization merger. Should a bank be tied to such a powerful combined organization?

Brendan Buck, spokesperson for House Speaker John Boehner, said, "American small businesses are more concerned about this administration's policies than from which building in Washington they originate."

The Commerce Department controls domestic and foreign business, trade, economic development, technology, entrepreneurship (job creation), and business development. The Commerce Secretary, with a budget of $7.6 billion and 47,000 employees, also covers divisions such as Census Bureau and the National Institute of Standards and Technology.

The Export-Import Bank, the official U.S. export credit agency founded in 1934, finances the export of U.S. goods and services. The official export credit agency of the United States, the Export-Import Bank has a budget of $89.9 million and 391 employees. Export-Import Bank does not compete with private sector lenders and guarantees loans from U.S. banks to foreign businesses that buy U.S. made products.

The U.S. House of Representatives delayed a long-term reauthorization of the Export-Import Bank and the decision to raise the lending cap to $135 billion from the current $100 billion limit.

"Airlines of America (AFA), the trade union that represents leading U.S. carriers, insist that Congress make fundamental changes to how the bank operates as part of any increase in the lending cap. The group argues that the bank finances loans to foreign carriers at favorable terms unavailable to domestic carriers, putting U.S. airlines at a competitive disadvantage." Foreign airlines with investor grade credit rating should secure financing from other banks, not the Export-Import Bank. (USA Today)

General Electric's CEO Jeffrey Immelt and Boeing's James McNerney wrote to House leaders that failure to increase the lending cap could lead to the loss of thousands of U.S. jobs. Boeing is arguing that the Export-Import Bank terms help Airbus.

Obama's administration supports the higher cap. The President cited the Export-Import bank for funding a multibillion-dollar deal for Indonesia Lion Air to buy 230 Boeing jets. A $636 million direct loan from the Export-Import Bank to finance the sale by Siemens Energy of gas and steam turbines to be installed in Saudi Arabia was hailed as a success of "in-sourcing" 825 jobs in North Carolina. I could be mistaken but Saudi Arabia is awash in oil money and Siemens is a corporation with high credit rating that can borrow money from the private sector, not from a taxpayer-sponsored bank.

"Reauthorizing the bank and expanding its lending cap is an administration priority, and we will continue to work closely with Congress to get this done," said Amy Brundage, White House spokeswoman. (USA Today)

Office of U.S. Trade Representative advises Obama on trade issues, develops and coordinates international trade policy and oversees negotiations. Ron Kirk, the U.S. Trade Representative, is Obama's Cabinet member since 2009. His office has a budget of $51.3 million and a staff of 227 employees.

Interestingly, Ron Kirk, the U.S. Trade Representative is also the Vice Chairman of the Board of Directors of the **Overseas Private Investment Corporation** (OPIC), a non-voting member of the **Export-Import Bank** Board of Directors, a member of the National Advisory Council on International Monetary and Financial Policies, and is on the Board of Directors of the Millennium Challenge Corporation. Millennium Challenge Corporation (MCC) is "an innovative and independent U.S. foreign aid agency that is helping lead the fight against global poverty." Isn't "global poverty" one of the favorite pet projects of liberals and UN Agenda 21?

It appears that Ron Kirk is a very influential man in three of the six government agencies that Obama wants to collapse into one.

Overseas Private Investment Corporation (OPIC) is presented in the mainstream media as helping U.S. businesses to establish a presence overseas. In actuality, they lead the way to Sustainability and help the implementation of UN Agenda 21. The OPIC Annual Report of 2010 states that "OPIC support projects that:

- Are environmentally and socially sustainable
- Are compatible with low- and no-carbon economic development
- Respect human rights, including the rights of workers and affected communities

- Avoid or provide mitigation and compensation for any negative impacts
- Provide timely project information to affected people
- Are undertaken in countries that are taking steps to adopt and implement laws that extend internationally recognized worker rights"

It appears that OPIC is more concerned with implementation of UN Agenda 21, low- and no-carbon economic development, thus eliminating fossil fuels, and international worker rights.

According to the Overseas Private Investment Corporation (OPIC) environmental and social policy, "OPIC and its partners and stakeholders work together to further the common aim of bringing sustainable prosperity to developing countries around the world," at the expense of U.S. economy and its citizens. It appears that this corporation, created in 1971, with a budget of $54.9 million and 215 employees is busy leading the way to UN Agenda 21 sustainability and elimination of fossil-fuel based economy.

The U.S. Trade and Development Agency (USTDA) gives grants to open emerging markets for increased exports of U.S. manufactured goods and services. Since our net exports, exports minus imports, is usually a negative number and thus a drag on Gross Domestic Product (GDP), the Trade and Development Agency's work with its $50 million budget and 50 employees has little positive impact on U.S. net exports. We have imported more than we have exported for years and the trend is not likely to change.

The agency claims that they have identified $3.6 billion of U.S exports directly attributable to USTDA-funded activities. The agency also boasts that for every dollar spent by the agency, USTDA's export measure grew to over $58. It is not clear how they arrived statistically at such a claim. The agency's projects focus on clean energy, transportation, telecommunications, and environmental services. This leaves out agriculture and other manufacturing sectors.

The Small Business Administration oversees the U.S. small businesses that "create 90 percent of new jobs and receive 23 percent of all federal contracts congressionally mandated by the Small Business Act." Karen Mills, the SBA administrator, would be elevated to Cabinet-level rank, an insignificant and deceptive move. Instead, the SBA's budget should be increased substantially and federal program significantly for America's main job creator.

As the evidence clearly shows, President Obama's attempt to merge six federal agencies into one is just a smoke screen for other agendas – it is not about streamlining government, saving $300 million a year for ten years, or just a transparent attempt at getting re-elected. More complicated relationships, interests, and outcomes are at stake.

Guantanamo Care Trumps Obamacare

Four hundred air miles from Miami, Florida is the oldest overseas U.S. Naval base in a country with which U.S. does not maintain diplomatic relations, Cuba. In 1903, U.S. leased 45 square miles of land and water at Guantanamo Bay for use as a coaling station and later as a refueling station.

The treaty was ratified and signed by both governments in Havana in December 1903 for $2,000 gold coins per year. In 1934, the lease was renewed by granting Cuba and its trading partners free access through the bay and the payment of $4,085 in actual dollars, not gold. To end the lease, both U.S. and Cuba must agree or the U.S. must abandon the base property.

Relations remained stable until the Cuban revolution in the late 1950's. Since January 1, 1959, the territory outside the base remains off-limits to civilians and U.S. service members. Official diplomatic relations with Cuba were cut off by President Eisenhower in January 1961. Some Cubans sought refuge on the base. Relations have been strained with the Castro government.

Of the original 380 who were allowed to stay and work on the base, there are 30 remaining. Of the 3,500 commuters in 1959 who were allowed to leave communist Cuba each morning and return in the evening through the North East Gate, only two remain today. They take retirement checks each month to the Cubans who retired from the Naval Station.

Thousands of Haitian refugees were processed through the Guantanamo base over the years during the violent coup of 1991 and the earthquake in 2010. Asylum seekers who make it across the border by land or intercepted at sea by Coast Guard vessels live temporarily in migrant facilities on base until are processed to third-party countries in Latin America.

The Naval Station has a self-sufficient base, which houses 5,337 people, mostly civilians and 2,103 military. A desalination plant produces

1.2 million gallons of water per day and the power plant 350,000 kilowatt-hours of electricity per day.

The Naval Station is separated by Guantanamo Bay and it can be accessed by AMC Rotator flights that land on the Leeward side of the base. The bay can be crossed by utility boat and ferry to the Windward side of the base where the prison is located.

In the wake of 9/11, the base started to incarcerate individuals captured by the U.S. military during execution of the War on Terror. The first prisoners arrived at Guantanamo Bay on January 11, 2002.

The "enemy combatants," a term coined by the Bush administration, have the legal status of unlawful combatants without protections under the Geneva Conventions. After legal fighting, the DOJ dropped in March 2009 the term "enemy combatant" from its legal lexicon and "established a new criterion for detention that did not rely on the Authorization for the Use of Military Force passed by Congress in September 2001."

President Obama called for the closure of Guantanamo Bay detention facility and signed an Executive Order that called for closure by January 22, 2010. Many detainees were released to countries like Spain, France, Austria, Tunisia, Portugal, Ireland, Hungary, Germany, Italy, Albania, Latvia, Switzerland, Belgium, Afghanistan, Yemen, and Slovakia.

Controversy over the proper venue to try such individuals captured on the battlefield dragged on. The DOJ wanted the detainees tried in federal court in New York. Congress halted plans to close Guantanamo Bay by giving final approval to a defense-spending bill, which blocked detainees from being transferred to the U.S. President Obama signed the Ike Skelton National Defense Authorization Act of 2011, which banned the use of funds to transfer Guantanamo detainees into the U.S.

Holder announced that defendants would be tried before a military commission, thus ending in April 2011 Obama's plan to try the accused 9/11 conspirators in federal courts.

On its tenth anniversary, Guantanamo Bay still houses 171 detainees down from 550 in 2005 and 779 in 2002. The detainees started a hunger strike on January 11, 2012, inspired by U.S. liberal activists with bleeding hearts for terrorists and criminals. Deutsche Welled interviewed the UK based legal group Reprieve, representing 15 detainees, about the "lack of hope that now pervades the camp."

These are no boy scouts, they range from bomb makers, bridge bombers, terrorist trainers, terrorist financiers, recruiters and facilitators, high value detainees who were Osama Bin Laden's guards, and at least five who are directly tied to the 9/11 attacks. Some detainees could have been released but no country wanted them. Some who had been released, committed new terrorist acts or returned to the battlefield. According to the Joint Task Force Guantanamo, "detainee assaults on the guard force occur on a regular basis."

According to the ACLU, our government spends $70 million annually to house the 89 prisoners who have been cleared for release. The Bush administration has released 532 prisoners while the Obama administration only 68. "Six prisoners died in custody by apparent suicide, one as a result of a heart attack, and one died of cancer." Military commissions at Gitmo spent $12 million in 2011. (ACLU)

Detainee programs include a social program (recreation, sports, prayers, family phone calls, mail), intellectual stimulation program (books, magazines, puzzles, newspapers, handheld electronic games, movies, satellite television), an instructional program (literacy, second language classes, art classes, computer classes, personal finance and business), a library with more than 25,000 titles, newspapers and magazines in 15 different languages, video games, DVDs, CDs, and a full-time librarian.

Living conditions exceed what is required by the Geneva Convention: Three meals a day that meet cultural dietary conditions and special diets, shelter, clothing, personal hygiene items, prayer beads, rugs, copies of the Quran in the native language of people from 40 countries, and mail. Detainees are visited by the Red Cross quarterly.

The most interesting aspect of the camp is health care. Medical services are available to detainees around the clock, seven days a week. Prisoners are treated in a dedicated medical facility with state-of-the-art equipment and expert medical staff of more than 100 people. There are 20 inpatient beds, physical therapy, pharmacy, radiology, and a single-bed operating room. Intensive care is offered at the Naval Station hospital and specialists can be flown in. A separate facility offers mental health care. Immunizations are given to detainees because none was available in their home countries. Prosthetic limbs are provided and cancerous tumors removed.

As you contemplate the coming rationing of health care in Obamacare, consider Guantanamo care: there is one medical staff for every two detainees and one primary care provider for approximately 45 detainees. The U.S. national average is one primary care provider for every 880 citizens.

As you wait eight hours to see an emergency room doctor, weeks to see a general practitioner, or six months to get an appointment with a specialist, examine Guantanamo Care: 129,000 meds dispensed annually; 4,650 sick call visits; 3,600 provider appointments; TB screenings conducted via the most accurate method available; colon cancer screening; 10 colonoscopies; 370 annual dental procedures; 470 radiology and physical therapy services; numerous consultations in cardiology, gastroenterology, neurology, radiology, urology, dermatology, audiology, orthopedics, ophthalmology, optometry, podiatry, and pulmonology. (Joint Task Force Guantanamo)

Can we afford to keep Guantanamo open? Can we afford to close it? Based on the valuable information obtained from various detainees, details that saved innumerable lives, the nature of the dangerous individuals, and the cost associated with Gitmo's maintenance, the questions seem difficult to answer.

Liberal Twisted Logic - Why Gas is Expensive

Recently, two Washington Post writers, in a half-page spread resplendent with meaningless pie charts and graphs that even a high school student would laugh off, failed miserably to explain, "Why we feel pain at the pump."

The two "progressive thinkers" stated that the perception that gas prices are soaring must be misleading because gas prices have soared before. Yes, we are feeling the pain, 71% of us, according to their poll, but the portion of income spent on gas is "relatively small." I am not sure about you, but spending $400 per month to fill up my gas tank is not an insignificant percentage of the average middle class family's disposable income; it may represent a car payment, a mortgage payment for some, and the food budget for the month, or the prescription bill.

Lutz Kilian, a quoted economics professor at the University of Michigan, apparently believes that "results do not provide any reason for panic." If I have to choose between food and fuel for my car to go to work, it is time to panic.

Dan Ariely from Duke said that the worry over gas prices is a "textbook example of an 'absolutely irrational' reaction." Only in the liberal universe of conflicted minds is the fear of $4-6/gallon price for a commodity that drives everything in this economy an irrational reaction. It is irrational to write an article to defend the indefensible with drivel that is aimed at covering up Obama's failed energy policy.

The writers continue, "A small case of nerves at the pump, however, may not be all bad, not even for President Obama, who is getting the blame." Who else is to blame? The media dereliction of duty is unbelievable. Price "spikes" are good, in their opinion, because it results in less consumption and "stokes interest in alternative sources of energy – key Obama issues."

I cannot wait until we develop enough cheap and affordable wind and solar energy to power our cars and industries, and I am being sarcastic. In the meantime, let us shut down coal and oil so we can return to the dark ages because a small group of individuals in power thinks it is the best for the majority. At the same time, China, India, and Russia are polluting away.

The suffering of the population from increased prices on all goods and services due to higher energy prices is not important to liberals as long as Obama is painted in a positive light. It is not about the American people, our country, and the economy, it is always about Obama.

We are noticing the high gasoline prices because "gas is sold by itself" and the price of the product is listed in BIG numbers. "You can't help but notice the price." In a liberal's mind, the fact that it costs $80 to fill a tank with gasoline is inconsequential, if they would only list the price in smaller letters, we would not be so upset.

As we watch the meter for five minutes, we see the price add up to the final total and we begin to panic, the writers continue. However, we do not panic when electricity adds up outside on a meter. I have news for mentally challenged liberals who refuse to understand the true cause of high prices – deliberate presidential plans and administrative incompetence.

Ariely said, "The meter for your electrical bill is outside the house usually, you have no idea how to read it, you don't stand next to it, and you pay only in retrospect."

Whether I see a gas pump run to a high dollar total in front of my eyes or I am presented with a huge electric bill at the end of the month, I still panic. I panic because it is real money that I have to earn by giving up my free time. When I give up more of my free time, I become a slave to someone else's failed decisions and policies. I become a slave because my time on this earth is limited.

It is gas money that I would not have to spend had the President not imposed a seven-year moratorium on domestic drilling in the Gulf while allowing foreign nations to drill in our own back yard. It is real money that the Fed has debased by printing too much - too much money, chasing too few goods, a direct result of out-of-control spending by this administration.

Using more flawed logic, Ariely said that "if you just bought one gallon, you might not remember how much it cost." Really? If I have to pay $5 for one gallon of gas that I used to pay $1 for, I would now not notice that it costs five times as much?

"If you bought 24 yogurts every time, you would probably

become more sensitive about the price per yogurt." This analogy is so insane; I cannot believe this person is actually teaching at Duke. Last time I checked at Sam's Club, it is vastly cheaper to buy a larger box of yogurt than it is to buy in smaller quantities. Furthermore, we consume yogurt one small container at a time, our stomachs can only handle so much yogurt. By contrast, an engine needs an exact amount of fuel to run, let's say 15 miles to the gallon. I cannot tamper with this fuel efficiency. I can drive slower perhaps but I cannot control the flow of traffic that causes my car to burn off more or less fuel.

Ariely calls fuel consumption the "pain of paying" because we pay and consume immediately. If we somehow had our tanks filled at night by some invisible presence as we slept and we got a monthly bill, we would not be so upset. Really? Almost $500 a month for gas is as painful to a consumer whether it is presented in increments or as a sum-total.

I can only summarize that Dr. Savage was right when he wrote, "Liberalism is a mental disorder." This faux journalism is media bias and gross dereliction of duty.

The Loons are Running the Asylum

We have always had crazy people, citizens lacking common sense, the misinformed, the ignorant, the purposeful deceptive, but we never used to put them in charge, until now. We are turning into **europameristan** because we think, it is not happening yet in our own back yards, neighborhoods, or towns.

We shake our heads in disbelief, joke about it, talk about it, write about it, while we are losing ground every day to a minority fringe bent on destroying everything around us and installing their ideas of civilized society: anarchy, socialism, Marxism, fascism, and Islamism.

Certain areas of the country that do not represent America elect politicians like Barbara Boxer who make damaging policy for the rest of the country. She said, "Climate deniers in this country are endangering humankind." In reality, the global warming hoax group is purposefully trying to destroy our economy by imposing United Nations mandated taxes on the United States, carbon taxes earmarked for third world dictatorships.

Boxer tried unsuccessfully to pass cap and trade after bullying Roy Spencer during his testimony on cap and trade. "She did not allow him to finish any sentence that she did not want to hear. She displayed no tact, class, or understanding of the scientific issues, making trite and embarrassing comments of a global warming cheerleader."

We allow Wall Street Occupiers to create chaos, filth, disease, and destruction in our cities in the name of democracy in action, freedom of speech, and political correctness. They want anarchy, chaos, drugs, unions, free trade, no borders, free food, free housing, free school, free cars, free gasoline, free day care, free clothes, free perennial vacations, and free health care, all paid for by the producing "evil capitalists."

We allow mainstream media to guide and control everything in this country because they know best what is good for the rest of the United States: socialism and Marxism, perennial dependency on government.

We permit the indoctrination of our children in schools into the leftist agenda of globalism, environmentalism, diversity, socialism, and communism.

We allow third world dictatorships at the United Nations to control our land, water, and energy use via UN Agenda 21 and carbon credit tax in the name of social justice necessitated by a faux man-made global warming.

The head master of a second grade school in the United Kingdom cut off the heat to an entire primary school during the coldest day in December to assuage his environmental guilt over his carbon footprint. The temperatures dipped to 1 degree Celsius while students shivered and were unable to perform their tasks. Parents were furious that this man chose to "save the planet" at the expense of their children's misery.

Al Gore, politicians, the rich Marxist advocates and communism-loving Hollywood fire up their jets or taxpayer provided jets to go on shopping sprees, vacations, and other leisurely activities with total disregard for pollution or their carbon footprint. Yet we are expected and forced to alter our life styles fundamentally in order to fit into their agenda of rolling back life to middle ages.

The globalists invented the measurement of carbon footprint and water footprint for the masses but the oligarchs in power are exempted from such life style changes. They can pollute away. Entire countries can stop their economic activities and it would barely nullify a few days of China's polluting industries.

We allow the federal government to replace parents and parental responsibilities. Detroit schools want to remain open during the Christmas holidays with the stated purpose to offer three meals a day to students and food baskets to their families. We do have food stamp programs in place and food banks, we do not need to keep schools open at great taxpayer expense. It is absolute insanity!

We allow TSA to dehumanize and humiliate us at airports in the name of air travel safety, an idea developed by progressives to better control mass transit. If we refuse the highly intrusive scanners, total strangers who seem to enjoy their newfound power are eager to molest us during pat downs.

"Sen. Susan Collins blasted the Defense Department for classifying the Fort Hood massacre as workplace violence and suggested political correctness is being placed above the security of the nation's

Armed Forces at home."

We allow voter fraud, political corruption, and squandering of our Treasury in the name of fairness, equity, social justice, and re-distribution of wealth. We are shamed and bullied into believing that protesting the corruption makes us bigots and racists.

We bailed out European banks that made irresponsible loans to irresponsible countries like Greece, Italy, Spain, and Portugal who spent lavishly on social programs while expecting the "dumb and ignorant" U.S. to be the military protector and policeman of the world.

Bernanke acknowledged that the Fed "loaned" $7.7 trillion to banks in 2008. Congress had "no idea to whom these loans were made." Bernanke claimed that he "saved the world from total catastrophe."

We bailed out national and international banks that were "too big to fail" because they bundled bad loans with good ones on the forced direction of Freddie Mac and Fannie Mae. Christopher Dodd, Barney Frank, and Maxine Watters assured us that both institutions were solid. Acorn and the Democrats picketed the homes of bankers to shame them into giving out mortgages to those unqualified who could not pay back the loans. If bankers refused, they were "racists and bigots."

We bailed out EU countries through the International Monetary Fund because our regime does not want socialism to fail before the 2012 elections. The beloved socialist pet of the Democrats and this administration is floundering once again.

We are allowing the destruction of the best healthcare in the world, making the U.S. into the socialist utopia in which thousands of people will die untreated because of rationing of care, disregard for human life, gross negligence, and government malpractice.

Only in an insane world would people believe that adding 30 million more patients to the health care pool would make medical care better.

Only in a utopian world makes sense to bankrupt a country in order to fund socialized health care that is a disaster anywhere else it has been tried or is currently used.

The sane majority is allowing the fringe minority to dictate how we live, eat, drink, travel, worship, and ultimately what and how we think.

Only a deliberately blind populace would commit cultural, religious, political, and economic suicide by allowing a Marxist minority to control 306 million people with political correctness and lawlessness.

The current regime has destroyed jobs, homes, investments, and health care, yet the President is still the only one who can save us? How many more radical activists can we afford to put on the judicial bench in the next four years? How many more progressives can we afford to put on the Supreme Court in the next presidential term?

Our President is criticizing the Internet as a job killer in banking and phone industries, trying to excoriate the economic sector for the lack of job creation under his watch. People understand that Congress and Obama's policies have caused the severe economic downturn. There is no denying it. He should know that Internet activity accounts for 21 percent of GDP growth.

The class warfare intensified with the tired rhetoric that the rich must pay their fair share in taxes. "T. Boone Pickens has paid $665 million in income taxes since age 70." Forty-seven percent of the population does not pay any federal taxes yet receive earned income tax credit. How much more "something for nothing" should they get?

If you do not own stock in a corporation, why do you care how much the stockholders decide to pay their "fat cats?" They are not responsible for your financial problems. You may have made poor choices in life. You may have chosen to drop out of school, or you may have chosen unwisely education in fields that are not employable. It is not the corporate world's fault for your unlucky choices. Politicians are at fault because they made the laws, funded them, and accepted campaign contributions from corporations.

People are weary of the tired out excuse that Obama inherited everything from Bush. George Bush's economic policies set a record of fifty plus months of job creation. Bush asked Congress 17 times, starting in 2001, to stop Fannie Mae and Freddie Mac because it was financially risky for the U.S. economy.

On January 3, 2007 the Democrats took over the Senate and Congress. On that day, the Dow Jones Industrial Average closed at 12,621.77, the GDP growth was at 3.5 percent, and the unemployment rate was 4.5 percent. Barney Frank took over the House Financial Services Committee and Chris Dodd took over the Senate Banking Committee. Fifteen months later we had an economic meltdown in the Banking and Financial Services.

Democrats controlled the budget process for 2008, 2009, 2010, 2011 and they still have not passed a budget. Nancy Pelosi and Harry Reid bypassed George Bush entirely, passing continuing resolutions to keep government running until Obama took office. In 2009 they passed a massive omnibus spending bill to complete the budget.

"The deficit Democrats did inherit was the 2007 deficit, the last of the Republican budgets, the lowest deficit in five years, and the fourth straight decline in deficit spending." Since Obama was an Illinois Senator, he should say, "I inherited a deficit that I voted for and then I voted to expand that deficit four times since my inauguration, to the highest level in U.S. history."

There is organized and well-planned chaos coming from all directions at unrelenting speed. I am not sure how much longer this country can survive at this rate of insanity. We have become a threadbare carpet held together by very thin strings, threatening to break at any moment if we do not handle it gently. The sane majority must prevail.

Misinformation 101 – The Jobs Report

My husband and I were browsing through a bookstore today. I spotted a Barack Obama, The Out of Office Countdown Calendar. I read the title to him and a woman's voice piped from behind, "Isn't this sad?"

I turned around to see the source of the remark and repeated, "Sad?" She replied, "Yes, very sad, as Martin Luther wrote, better to vote for a good Turk than a bad Christian. You do know who Martin Luther was, don't you? Not Dr. Martin Luther King."

At this point, I was trying very hard to keep my composure and ignore the insults and assaults to my intelligence. I told her, she was mistaken, and I walked away. Fighting with an ignorant liberal in the middle of a bookstore was not my idea of a fun Saturday afternoon. In the meantime, my husband disappeared behind several bookshelves.

Like any bold and obnoxious liberal, the woman followed me, spewing typical progressive non-sense about the evil Christians and the good Muslims who were slaughtered mercilessly. I did not turn this time, gesturing for her to go away.

We are flooded with lies by the MSM, the progressive academics, the Obama crowd, the Democrat and RINO politicians; the last place I expected to encounter indoctrination into communist talking points was at my local bookstore.

Delusional pro-Muslim and anti-Christian liberals are everywhere but particularly concentrated in the northeast. An informational takeover and coup of our values and of our country is waged by a small, atheist, anti-American, pro-Muslim minority with an agenda to destroy everything that millions of patriotic Americans have created in 235 years of exceptional history.

Spreading misinformation and communist propaganda is the Modus Operandi of liberals. If sleepy Americans hear the same lies repeated many times, they will believe them to be true.

The Department of Labor released its weekly jobs report, claiming that 200,000 jobs were created, much more than the 150,000 needed monthly to accommodate a growing population. According to the Bureau of Labor Statistics, the unemployment rate dropped from 8.7 percent to 8.5 percent. What they failed to mention was the fact that over 20 million Americans are unemployed, part-time employed, or no longer counted in the labor force. BLS massaged the data down to 8.1 percent unemployment. By the time President Obama is re-elected, the job report numbers will be well within the limits of full-employment. Everyone unemployed will no longer be counted and will be on the government dole.

The labor force has been traditionally 156 million workers. If we do the simple math, the unemployment rate is higher overall. Some counties in California reported 20 percent unemployment. Areas around Detroit, Michigan claimed 40 percent unemployment.

Statistics can be tampered and manipulated to reveal any talking points an individual wishes to make, particularly if a lot is at stake, in this case, the re-election of a failing President. Data is revised up and down all the time in this administration, particularly up, after the intended euphoria of good news has passed. To say that statistics and data reported in the past three years have been disingenuous is an understatement.

The basic unemployment data comes from a monthly survey of 60,000-80,000 households conducted by the U.S. Bureau of Labor Statistics. The results of the survey are extrapolated to the entire U.S. labor force.

The "elephant-in-the-room" problem is that a large percentage of the unemployed are no longer counted if they have not sought work during the previous four weeks, the people no longer exist. These are the discouraged workers. When they give up searching for a job, they are out of the labor force, and the official unemployment rate declines. The magnitude of the problem is thus underestimated by the existence of this "hidden" or "disguised" unemployment.

We are in a severe cyclical unemployment phase driven by poor and inadequate economic policies of the current administration, the expensive prospect of Obamacare, and by federal regulations that limit and sometimes prohibit job creation.

I am not surprised that liberals/progressives/communists misinform Americans. I dislike the attempt to rewrite history and reality on a daily basis. Martin Luther never lived under a Muslim ruler. There is no evidence that he ever said, "I'd rather be ruled by a competent Turk than an incompetent Christian." Scholarship disputes the claim made by Hubert Morken in "Pat Robertson – Where He Stands," on p. 42 in which he attributes the comment to Martin Luther without any citation. As you saw, the liberal stranger I encountered had totally transformed the supposed quote to tailor her agenda. I studied Martin Luther, his 95 theses, I speak German, and I never saw such a quote.

I take any information from liberal and conservative leaders or individuals, in reference to historical, literary, political, geographical, or economic data with a large spoon of salt.

What Would You Do as President After Obama?

The historian Livy wrote about the Roman statesman, Lucius Quinctius Cincinnatus, who answered the call of duty to his country in a time of crisis.

In 458 BC, Cincinnatus was named dictator of Rome for six months to rescue a consular army surrounded by the Aequi on Mount Algidus. When duty called, he was working on his small farm. He accepted the request of the Senate to lead the Roman Army. He defeated the enemy in a single day and returned triumphantly to Rome. Cincinnatus maintained his power for fifteen days, long enough to return Rome to normalcy. He then resigned and went back to his farm.

Cincinnatus was admired for his lack of ambition although he was consul in 460 and 438 BC, and for his selfless patriotism.

If you were called to duty to save our country, what would you do, what would be the first thing you would tackle in order to save our floundering economy? I asked random conservatives and libertarians, and developed their brief answers.

I would increase economic freedom by making it much easier to start a business. Current regulations are so arcane, vending, zoning, taxation, that it is hard to maintain or start a new business.

I would control immigration by putting troops at the border in addition to current border patrols. I would start by putting three divisions on the southern border, two infantry and one mechanized. The fence is not a good deterrent as many have proven that it can be easily escalated, cut through, or crawled underneath. I would assign the border control to both the federal and state governments. I would give states the right to confront illegal aliens.

I would reverse abortion laws since the demographics show that population birth rates in most western nations are below replacement values. Western civilizations would disappear without 2.1 babies per family. Sadly, a disproportionate number of black babies are being aborted in the U.S.

I would reinstate "don't ask, don't tell" because soldiers have not been consulted if openness increases or decreases troop morale. Liberals have decided for the majority.

I would reform the tax code to make it uniform and less burdensome on small business. I would prefer, however, to institute a flat tax. It works very well in several countries that are prospering economically.

I would repatriate all profits of large companies and make them pay tax on all their earnings overseas. I would audit all major Wall Street firms and particularly the Federal Reserve System because it does not answer to anybody. I would make the Fed prove that our gold reserves at Fort Knox are intact.

I would pass a budget amendment forcing Congress to pass a budget. It has been three years since the Democrat-controlled Congress passed a budget.

I would institute term limits for Congressmen and Congresswomen. To serve one's country was not meant to be a life-long career of corruption, bribery, and theft, becoming rich at the trough of government. I would appoint a commission to identify all powers not specifically enumerated in the Constitution and fight relentlessly to excise them from government.

I would reduce business tax rate to about 25 percent, eliminate deductions, and repeal most of the new regulations in the Dodd-Frank Wall Street Act.

I would cut EPA's solar expenditures and all regulations that are stifling economic growth and development and kill jobs in many sector industries, including mining, oil exploration, land use, and water use. Solar expenditures, as proven lately, are likely to bankrupt us. In spite of four highly touted solar panel manufacturers going out of business, four more Obama supported crony capitalist ventures in the solar panel industry have received $4.7 billion dollars for the advancement of his "green" industry agenda.

I would cut Social Security; eliminate the U.S. Department of Health and Human Services and its budget, including Medicare and Medicaid, which are in trouble financially.

"I would defund and repeal Obamacare" was the most popular choice of respondents. The monstrous 3,000 page bill that nobody read, nobody discussed, and Nancy Pelosi asked that be passed first before we knew what was in it, is the elephant in the closet that is already draining billions.

Doctors are busy implementing and establishing the bureaucracy required to run Obamacare. It has already resulted in unusual delays in treatment. None of the promises made by Obama turned out to be true so far.

Premium costs for most families have already gone up 9 percent to $15,073 in 2011, the largest increase since 2005. Single premiums have gone up 8 percent. People were shocked that their adult children premiums, no annual caps on benefits, and no copays for preventive care were not free, they added to the premium.

Health care premiums did not decrease by $2,500 per family as promised. According to Kaiser Family Foundation, "premiums increased significantly faster than workers' wages (2.1%) and general inflation (3.2%)."

"If you like your current plan, you can keep it." Many Americans, who can afford and like their current plan, will not be able to keep it. Fifty-six percent of employees will be able to keep their plans under the "grandfathered protection." The Kaiser Family Foundation survey says, "Numerous firms responded that being grandfathered was administratively difficult and it would limit the firm's flexibility in the future."

"Small business tax credits would encourage employers to provide coverage." "With that savings, employers may be able to cover an additional worker or hire that extra employee they've needed." The Kaiser survey says that only "fifteen percent of non-offering small firms with 3-49 employees considered health insurance because of the tax credit."

The 1,472 waivers given to crony employers and unions because they could not afford the premiums will expire in 2014. Mid- and large-size employers will have to provide "the essential benefit package" or pay a $2,000 fine. The fine is so small when compared to the premiums that middle and high earners will be forced into health exchanges and lower income workers into Medicaid.

Medicaid only pays 86 cent of every dollar, forcing doctors and hospitals to pass the cost to privately insured patients, driving up the cost of premiums for them. Obamacare will increase Medicaid enrollment by one third in 2014 and two thirds of the currently uninsured will be placed on Medicaid. The cost of all this Medicaid expansion will come from the higher private health insurance premiums.

Premiums will also go up because of the rising costs of

healthcare. Americans spend, including out-of-pocket, $7,538 a year, according to the Organization for Economic Cooperation and Development. U.K., Norway, and Sweden spend $2,995. (Betsy McCaughey)

Respondents believed that SOX should be repealed. Sarbanes Oxley Act, passed July 2002, known as SOX, an act of corporate responsibility, to protect investors by "improving the accuracy and reliability of corporate disclosures, made pursuant to the securities laws, and for other purposes," was enacted after numerous scandals such as Enron and WorldCom. SOX does not apply to privately held corporations.

Supporters believe SOX improved the confidence of fund managers and investors in the veracity of corporate financial statements. Opponents argue that SOX introduced a very complex regulatory environment into the U.S. financial markets thus reducing America's international competitiveness against foreign financial service providers.

The respondents were extremely knowledgeable and offered viable solution to our economic crises. No matter which president will replace Obama in 2012, his/her job will be extremely difficult to fix our disintegrating economy, which the Democrats, aided by many Republicans, and Obama's misguided economic policies have devastated.

Are You Better Off Than You Were 14 Trillion Dollars Ago?

The conservative majority protests by millions under the Tea Party banner were generally ignored by the media. The Taxed Enough Already (TEA) message was distorted, maligned, and astro-turfed. The liberal minority protested violently and the media displayed them ad nauseam as if they are the only citizens in this country. Hate speech replaced political correctness with the same end game, to silence the free speech of conservatives.

Sharia Law was introduced in parts of the country although it is incompatible with our Constitution and our legal system. We seem to be unable to stop its advancement and promotion by a small, well organized, and funded minority.

United Nations Agenda 21 has been stealthily introduced since 1992 at the state and local levels and it is now in the full phase of implementation The last three years have turned our country upside down politically, economically, racially, morally, fiscally, and internationally. I no longer recognize the U.S. that many citizens around the globe admired, aspired to emulate, dreamed to visit, owed their freedom to, and considered big brother in times of need, disaster, and danger.

We have lost NASA space program and our leading edge in space. We are now left with renting a chair on the Chinese or Russian flights, we are the poor cousin who does not own a car and must pay for a ride.

The emotional and hollow "hope and change" for utopia has turned into a nightmare that some of us recognized from past painful experience. We have lost our triple rating as a financial super power, we are a nation with shady credit and insurmountable debt. It threatens our national security.

We have a housing crisis caused and manipulated by Democrat Congressmen like Barney Frank, Chris Dodd, and Maxine Watters who kept assuring President Bush that we did not need to clean up Fannie Mae and Freddie Mac. We did not need to reign in the forced lending of expensive homes to poor people who did not intend to pay them back. Democrats told us that it was unfair to deny mortgages to people with shady credit.

The Administration nationalized Chrysler and GM, violating private contracts, shafting shareholders and bondholders to the benefit of unions and a foreign corporation, Fiat.

Obama took over college lending with the intention of telling students where to go to school, what to study, where to work when they graduated, and how much money they could make.

Banks who were forced to make bad mortgage loans failed and were bailed out with taxpayer money. Even foreign owned insurance companies received our hard-earned dollars. We made investments in the oil industries of Brazil while preventing American companies from drilling.

This administration stopped giving FEMA funds for disaster relief to states that did not vote for Obama or Democrats. Some states were completely ignored in their hours of need, while others were turned down twice such as the Commonwealth of Virginia.

EPA issued stringent regulations responsible for the shutdown of coal-burning plants that generate electricity. The expressed purpose was to make electricity more expensive and discourage its use. Seventy thousand jobs were threatened in West Virginia due to excessive mining regulations.

Billions of dollars in grants were given to solar panel makers like Solyndra that eventually went bankrupt because they could not make the panels cheap enough to make the industry efficient in generating solar power. Presently solar energy is not going to be able to replace energy needs for the largest economy on earth.

The states of Arizona and Alabama were sued by the Justice Department for passing acts to enforce immigration laws. The federal government failed to protect our borders adequately.

The medical and health insurance system were nationalized by strong-arming Congress, bribing it, forcing the passage of a 3,000-page bill that nobody understood, read, or debated thoroughly as it should have been. In spite of the large citizen opposition, it passed in the dead of night.

Taxes were increased and imposed on the average American while stoking the masses with the lies of "tax the rich," "tax the corporate fat cats," "make them pay their fair share," "make Wall Street pay." Acorn played a pivotal role in intimidating CEOs into giving in to their demands by protests at their homes. Acorn helped register millions of non-existent citizens, dead voters, animals, and cartoon characters.

College students, who have no understanding of how the economy works or even care to understand how it works, were paid to protest and occupy Wall Street and other cities around the nation with money from SEIU, Daily Kos, Moveon.org, Soros, Van Jones, and other like-minded Marxist outlets. Defecating publicly in parks, stoned, drinking beer, and yelling non-sense, they appear to be the armies that Obama had promised in his pre-election speeches that will "fundamentally transform America" through a communist revolution.

America was not in need of change, it did not need fundamental transformation. The ardent supporters did not pay attention to the message. They were mesmerized by the charisma, the style, the youth, the skin color, and the empty suit promises from a man who never held a real job in his life, just like some of his voters who lived in their parents basements.

Protesting capitalism, while listening to music on iPods, using iphones, and other electronic devices invented by entrepreneurial Americans, paid malcontents asked for sleeping bags, food, doctors, medicine, and other goods produced by the free market capitalism.

We now have crony capitalism – only Obama's friends and donors need apply for special favors, grants, and stimuli. We had so many bailouts, grants, incentives and jobs programs. We have lost count of the billions wasted that lined the pockets of his supporters and Democrat campaign chests instead of fixing our infrastructure, our schools, roads, and bridges.

Unemployment is around twenty percent, not the deceptive nine percent reported in the media. There are almost 25 million unemployed, underemployed, and discouraged workers. This number represents 20 percent of our labor force of approximately 125 million Americans.

College graduates are beginning to wake up that they are not going to find the dream job they thought they were going to waltz into, making a six-figure salary just because they received a college degree in some esoteric field with no job openings or prospects. Nobody wants to start at the bottom and gain experience.

Government does not create jobs, it creates bureaucracies with despotic bureaucrats who take away and control more and more of our freedoms. Small businesses and corporations create jobs, the very corporations that are vilified constantly by Obama and his Democrats.

Obamacare has every employer on the edge about hiring. They are not sure what tax, regulations, and health insurance liabilities they will incur. Business and consumer confidence are at an all time low.

The Democrat-controlled Congress passed bills to regulate Wall Street and banks. They are now bearing fruit in the form of higher costs passed on to consumers. Are banks greedy? The greed comes from Congress and Obama's administration who want power, votes, and re-election contributions. Many bills Congress passed allowed businesses to move overseas, to reduce or eliminate their tax burden, and to make it easier hire foreign workers. Companies made generous campaign contributions to Congress.

The job czar, the head of GE, has moved some GE factories to other countries, citing higher demand and a better business environment. It is a blatant conflict of interest to have the head of GE tasked with the creation of American jobs.

Health insurance premiums have increased dramatically and many citizens will not be able to keep their insurance or their doctors as promised. We are losing the best medical care in the world because a few million people needed insurance – we are throwing the baby out with the bathwater instead of addressing the real problems such as tort reform and buying insurance across state lines.

We no longer have culture debates on various issues as we used to have under past presidents: abortion, animal rights, bilingual education, drugs, gun politics, multiculturalism, sexual education, stem cell research, law and order, media bias, moral apathy, feminism, secularism, and the death penalty. These debates are gone as if everything has been resolved and decided by the current regime and the liberal media.

. The Obama federal government has mandated a Sustainability plan for every department that includes green energy, land use, water use, green building, smart city growth, and green transportation. The end game is to confiscate private property by making it useless to the owner and forcing them into mixed use, high-rise tenements, five minutes from work and school by bike or walking.

Public transportation will replace our use of cars. In certain D.C. suburbs, roads are being narrowed to make driving and parking difficult or impossible. Maryland high school students cannot read or write well but they must pass an environmental literacy exam in order to graduate.

We are ruled by EPA and Department of Energy fiat rules and regulations that empower government bureaucrats to take our private wealth and re-distribute it to the poor in this country and around the globe in the name of social justice.

We have spent trillions of dollars on the War on Poverty and we have not made a dent into this perceived poverty. We have lost this war but the rhetoric of poverty gets louder and louder from the left.

Advisors to the White House want a population control plan because they think the planet is strained and there are just too many inhabitants. The herd must be culled through attrition or birth control because we are hurting the environment. We must become slaves and good stewards to the environment, giving land back to the wild according to the Wildlands Project.

Law and order is no longer enforced, as it should be, officers are looking away as vagrants/protesters occupy public and private areas for weeks but are allowed to stay because owners have ties to either the mayor's office or the elites in power in Washington. Voters were threatened and intimidated by baton yielding individuals who were not prosecuted.

The compliant media are open promoters of Marxism, no longer afraid to show their true socialist colors they have been hiding for years. Hollywood is promoting and advocating re-education camps for the rich who refuse to give up their wealth in excess of $100 million. If that fails, they are calling for the guillotine. Is this America we know and want?

Nobody respects us in the world anymore. People are shocked that we elected such overt Marxist incompetence in Washington. Where is the unconditional love of Obama's presidency going to bring us? He is disrespected more than many former presidents because his lavish spending has brought the rest of the world closer to the brink of financial meltdown and ruin.

Luckily, we do have a few items left in our arsenal of freedoms: our dignity, our guns, our voting rights, and freedom of speech and assembly. If they shut down the Internet, we can still meet and honor our duty to save and protect the Constitution and our country from destruction.

Alice in Wonderland - Further Down the Rabbit Hole

The United States experienced recently the most severe recession since the end of World War II. The housing collapse, the resulting economic downturn, TARP, and various bailouts and economic stimuli resulted in a rapid buildup in federal debt held by American taxpayers, 36 percent of GDP at the end of 2007, 62 percent of GDP at the end of 2010, and 100 percent of GDP at the end of 2011. Our national debt is $17 trillion, on par with gross domestic product.

Almost half of all Americans under the age of 30 do not have jobs. One in five men of working age is unemployed. Twenty-five percent of college graduates are without a job with no prospects in sight. There are 13.1 million unemployed Americans. We have lost track of discouraged workers.

We have a "progressive" and broken education system, a dwindling military, constant threats of terrorism, nuclear Iran, exploding entitlements and health care costs, illegal immigration problems, endemic government corruption, the Democrat-controlled Congress has not passed a budget in 1,000 days, crushing new regulations, the collapse of the Euro, the violence in Iraq after the departure of U.S. troops, to name just a few.

Our President continues to misrepresent America as strong, concentrating his vacuous teleprompting on class warfare, fairness, and massive tax and spending increases, vilifying the rich who "do not pay their fair share."

Emphasizing his campaign mantra of "hope and change," the President stated in his union address, "The executive branch also needs to change. Too often, it's inefficient, outdated, and remote. That's why I've asked this Congress to grant me the authority to consolidate the federal bureaucracy so that our government is leaner, quicker, and more responsive to the needs of the American people." Was not the intent of our Founding Fathers to balance powers by creating three distinct branches of government?

By guaranteeing equal outcomes for all Americans, regardless of one's merit, and encouraging mediocrity and sloth, this administration continues to de-develop America.

He made scant mention of Obamacare, its challenge in the Supreme Court, its bankrupting costs, Social Security crisis, energy crisis, the Solyndra scandal, the denial of the Keystone XL pipeline, the expensive and bogus green initiatives, and illegal "recess appointments" while Congress was not in recess.

The President forgot to mention his visit to Brazil in March 2011 to secure contracts for oil. "We want to work with you. We want to help with technology and support to develop these oil reserves safely, and, when you're ready to start selling, we want to be one of your best customers."

Petrobras, the state-controlled oil company will pump 4.9 million barrels a day by 2020 from an ultra-deep sea of oil. The President of Brazil signed instead contracts a month later with two state-owned Chinese companies. China had offered Petrobras a $10 billion loan in 2009 on the promise that Petrobras will ship oil to China for 10 years.

Curiously ignored was the fact that the U.S. is exporting for the first time in 62 years, gasoline. We started exporting gasoline in late 2008.

In case you are scratching your heads in bewilderment because you are paying $4 to $4.50 to fuel your car with Diesel or could be paying record high gas prices this year, consider this. The U.S demand for gas has dropped 10 percent (from 9.6 million barrels per day in 2007 to 8.8 million) and we have excess refining capacity.

Recssion, fuel-efficient vehicles, higher prices, use of ethanol as ingredient in gasoline, decline in travel, decline in use of jet fuel and Diesel, caused the drop in demand for gas. Prices should drop based on the supply-demand model, however, we are paying $100 per barrel of crude from OPEC countries.

We are still importing plenty of crude oil; we are dependent on foreign countries for over half the crude. However, we export gasoline now to Brazil, Mexico, and Chile where demand for gasoline is stronger. Shell, Exxon Mobil, BP, and Chevron are happy to refine crude to make gasoline for the rest of the world.

President Obama said in his State of the Union speech that the future of America is a "future where we're in control of our own energy, and our security and prosperity aren't so tied to unstable parts of the world." Yet he denied the Keystone pipeline XL days before, a pipeline that would have carried oil from Alberta, Canada to refineries on the U.S. Gulf Coast. At the same time, he squanders money on ephemeral green energy such as the bankrupt Solyndra, the faulty electric Volt that nobody wants to purchase, and expensive renewable energy.

Sen. Joe Manchin III (D- West Virginia) said, "President Obama's decision on the Keystone XL pipeline is a major setback for the American economy, American workers, and America's energy independence."

Obama could have created 20,000 shovel-ready jobs and 179,000 jobs by 2035 with the Keystone pipeline. He could have granted offshore oil leases – only one was given in 2011. He could have reversed the 40 percent reduction in oil and natural gas production on federal lands, a decade long drop.

Instead, the President announced in front of Cinderella's Castle his latest plan to create jobs by increasing tourism to the United States. He signed an Executive Order on January 19, 2012, "establishing visa and foreign visitor processing goals and the task force on travel and competitiveness." He also created another bureaucracy, Recreation.gov, the new Federal Interagency Council on Outdoor Recreation. Tapping tourism as a creator of American jobs, "This is the first time our country has had a national strategy and set goals for the amount of visitors we want to welcome." The interagency tourism and this quote were troubling on many levels.

During the week on January 25, 2012, 1,600 economic and political elites and 40 heads of states met in Davos, Switzerland for the 42nd World Economic Forum to find ways to reform capitalism because they found it "outdated and crumbling." Perhaps they are planning to replace it with *global crony capitalism.*

Preoccupied with the global economy in light of the downgrade of credit worthiness of 12 EU countries, including France, discussions centered on deficit of leadership in Europe, social responsibility, and environmental issues. The ever-present Occupiers protested the "self-proclaimed elites."

Our 236-year old monolithic sovereign rock called America had been chiseled away by domestic and international socialists/communists for the last hundred years. They are now sledge hammering big chunks from our rock of freedom. Why do we allow it? Why is a failed utopia so tantalizing to Americans?

ABOUT THE AUTHOR

A former Economics college professor with thirty years teaching experience, the author has the unique perspective of growing up under a communist totalitarian state and values the freedom and opportunity that capitalist America has given her. As a patriotic American citizen by choice, she warns of the daily assaults that are threatening the "shining city on the hill," and wants to stem the collapse before it is too late.

A weekly radio commentator, speaker, and senior columnist for Canada Free Press, Dr. Ileana Johnson Paugh uses her knowledge to continue educating thousands of readers and listeners. She speaks fluently several foreign languages. This skill gives her the opportunity to read the news as they happen around the globe.

Besides Economics, the author taught German, Italian, Latin, and Russian to students in a public college preparatory high school in the south. She does not hold a teaching license but has four advanced college degrees in various fields.

Her previous book, "Echoes of Communism," is available at Amazon in paperback and Kindle. A personal compilation of childhood experiences and becoming an American citizen by choice, "Echoes of Communism" describes the daily life in a totalitarian state from many non-romanticized vantage points: religion, superstitions, poverty, confiscation of property, social engineering, freedom of speech, and education.

The author can be reached through her web site, ileanajohnson.com and her Facebook author page, Dr. Ileana Johnson Paugh.

www.ingramcontent.com/pod-product-compliance
Lightning Source LLC
Chambersburg PA
CBHW070004300526
45794CB00001B/182